Ketogenic Diet With Intermittent Fasting For Rapid Weight Loss!

3 Books In 1

Special Edition

Table of Contents

Chapter 5: Ketogenic Main Course Recipes160

Chapter 6: Ketogenic Dessert Recipes......... 191

Introduction

I want to thank you and congratulate you for purchasing the book, *"Ketogenic Diet: Ketogenic Diet for Weight Loss and Amazing Energy"*.

This book contains **proven steps and strategies** on how to embark on a dietary journey that is guaranteed to revolutionize your health. In here you will discover actionable and practical information on how to lose fat and improve energy levels. If you have been on other types of diets before and have struggled to shed those pounds or even boost your energy levels, the Ketogenic diet will help you immensely.

So what is a Ketogenic diet? It is simply a diet where a person consumes foods that provide them with more fat, and very few carbs and proteins. In a Ketogenic diet, you get up to **90%** of your calories in form of fats, with the rest being split between the other two macronutrients.

The Ketogenic diet is aimed at causing a shift in the body's utilization away from glucose to fats. In other words, you are causing your body to burn fats rather than what it is normally used to – sugars. During this process, your liver produces substances known as **ketone bodies.**

A Ketogenic diet is very restrictive in terms of how many carbohydrates you are allowed to consume on a daily basis. This level is usually restricted to about **50 to 100 grams of carbs every day.** Carbohydrates have been identified as the cause of most of our society's dietary health issues. This is especially true for processed carbohydrates, which can be addictive and unhealthy. The truth is that most people aren't even aware that all those processed carbs they are eating are making them fat. **All the exercise in the world won't help you lose weight** if you are still consuming large quantities of foods laden with processed carbs. That is why the Ketogenic diet is specifically focused on minimizing the carbohydrate intake.

The quantity of fats and proteins you consume may vary somewhat, but what eventually makes a particular diet Ketogenic is the quantity of carbohydrates it contains. This may seem difficult for some people but it is precisely his measure that makes the Ketogenic diet so effective. Your body simply adapts to the new way of energy production with time. Many people have discovered that the

Ketogenic diet is able to help them **burn fat and increase their energy levels** in ways that other diets had failed to achieve.

If you have never heard of or tried the Ketogenic diet, then **this book will unravel it all in a simple and clear manner.** If you already know something about this diet, then this book will still benefit you by going deeper into some of the details that are often left out in other books. You will learn the brief history of the Ketogenic diet, discover what ketone bodies and ketosis really means, and how ketogenesis impacts your body. There are also some **great recipes** that you can sample in chapter 4. In chapter 5 we discuss about the **basic principles of ketogenic diet** and we share some important points about the daily routine and food shopping. Finally, we wrap up with some of the **misconceptions and mistakes** you need to avoid.

I hope you enjoy the book!

Free Bonus

I want to thank you for purchasing this book, hence I would like to give you a free gift in return. Click here or follow the link below to claim your free gift now.
Cheers!

http://eepurl.com/cRXcDf

Chapter 1: An Overview of the Ketogenic Diet

We all know that a normal diet consist of three macronutrients – carbohydrates, proteins, and fats. The human body generally takes the carbohydrates consumed and breaks it down into glucose, which is the simplest molecule of all. Whenever glucose is detected in the bloodstream, the pancreas automatically produces insulin, a hormone that serves a very important function. Insulin will either transport the glucose to the tissues that require energy at that time, or it may trigger storage of the glucose in form of fat to be used later when required. Glucose is the obvious choice for energy production in the body because it is the simplest and easiest molecule that the body can use when energy is required.

However, a Ketogenic diet advocates for a low carbohydrate intake and elevated fat consumption. One thing to note is that going on a Ketogenic diet and fasting are somewhat similar in terms of metabolic reactions. A Ketogenic diet mimics the metabolic effects of fasting, the main difference being that you will still be consuming food. The goal here is to force your body to produce its energy and meet its calorific demands by burning fats. In order to get to understand just how this entire process works, it is critical that we look at the inner workings of your metabolism.

The moment you stop eating carbohydrates, you will experience a decline in energy reserves. This will happen quickly because your body is used to getting glucose to satisfy its fuel demands. Your body will have no choice but to look for an alternative source of energy. The next best thing would be protein. The only problem with this is that it would lead to muscle wastage, which is something you don't want. Muscles are necessary for all kinds of motion, especially when you consider things from the fight-or-flight perspective.

One viable option is **free fatty acids (FFAs).** Almost all tissues in the body, with the exception of the brain and nervous system, can use free fatty acids. In such a scenario where the body no longer relies on glucose for energy, the brain and nervous system will have to use ketone bodies as an energy source. This is what is known as ketosis. Your body will shift from burning glucose to burning ketones.

Ketone Bodies

What are ketone bodies and where do they come from? Ketone bodies, or ketones, are produced from the partial breakdown of free fatty acids in the liver. When ketone bodies are broken down, the body is able to utilize them as a source of energy. It is important to state that ketosis is a natural process. There are times when you are low on blood sugar or feel as if you are starving, yet your vital organs like the brain still need to function. During such periods of time, ketones are the fallback plan to keep your critical body functions going.

It is also important to note that research has shown ketones to have a stimulating effect on the growth of neural paths within the brain. When your body undergoes ketosis, it is simply following a natural process that helps you burn off the excess fat while improving your cognitive function.

Ketone bodies are not just produced during periods of starvation. There are certain times when the body utilizes both ketones as well as available glucose in order to keep energy levels high. The ketones are used to ensure that there is enough energy for survival. Infants also depend on ketosis as their primary mode of survival. **Mother's breast milk** does not contain much glucose, but rather ketone bodies that are used to provide essential energy. As kids grow up, they are pushed to start consuming a diet that is filled with carbs and sugars. This is when all the unhealthy eating habits start, resulting in weight gain and low energy.

The reality is that a metabolism that burns fat is totally natural and safe. Ketosis has been tried and tested for years and the results speak for themselves. It can be used to treat disorders and is also a good lifestyle to adopt. Once you understand how the Ketogenic diet impacts your body, you will have taken a major step towards your overall health goals.

Ketosis

It is important to clarify the meaning of the term *ketosis* in order to remove any confusion that there may be regarding this term. In most cases, people make the mistake of confusing ketosis and another dangerous metabolic condition that affects diabetics, known as **ketoacidosis.** This condition will be discussed in the next section.

Ketosis can be referred t as a metabolic condition characterized by the burning of fat to generate energy for the body. Instead of breaking down glucose, the body breaks down fatty tissue into ketone bodies. This is what makes the Ketogenic diet one of the most effective ways to use up body fat and thus lose weight. When you start to consume more fats and reduce your carb intake, your body gets used to breaking down fats for energy production.

The moment your body adapts to burning fats that come from foods, it will also find it easier to metabolize the excess fatty deposits around your body. Ketosis as a metabolic process has also been found to repair some of the damage that a carbohydrate-laden diet inflicts on the body, for example, insulin sensitivity and poor metabolic functions. Ketosis is safe and can be used in the treatment of a number of ailments. Compared to taking different kinds of medicines your entire life, ketosis seems like a more sensible solution.

Ketoacidosis

This is a dangerous condition that normally afflicts people who are Type 1 diabetic. A person suffering from Type 1 diabetes suffers from low insulin production. They are also likely to have been consuming a diet filled with carbs for a very long time. Let's say that a healthy individual consumes a meal full of carbs. Naturally, the body will produce insulin to break down the complex carbs into glucose, to be used for energy production.

If a Type 1 diabetic eats the same meal as above, their body will go ahead and break down the carbs to glucose, but there's one problem. They are suffering from inadequate production of insulin. This means that they cannot break down the glucose for energy! The result is that they will eat all they want but they won't have any energy, thus forcing their body to turn to fat as an energy source.

Their body starts to break down fat into ketone bodies for use as n energy source. But therein lies another problem. Insulin is required to regulate the production of ketone bodies, but there simply isn't sufficient insulin to control the process of producing ketones. The result is an overproduction of ketones. Remember that ketones are derived from fatty acids, and from the name itself, you can tell that the body's PH will soon turn acidic. This is what leads to the condition known as ketoacidosis.

Ketoacidosis is characterized by symptoms such as inflammation, dehydration, and swollen brain tissues. This condition can be potentially fatal if not caught and treated in time. For people who are not diabetic, there is nothing to worry about regarding the Ketogenic diet. As long as your body is able to produce enough insulin to control the production of ketone bodies and maintain your health, ketoacidosis is not something to worry about. That is why it is crucial that you consult your doctor before you begin the Ketogenic diet. Even a person suffering from Type 1 diabetes can go on a Ketogenic diet, as there are safe ways to make the diet work for such a patient. For example, if you are taking insulin replacement hormones, you can be able to go on a Ketogenic diet. As always, the most important step is to first confirm with your physician.

History of the Ketogenic Diet

The Ketogenic diet is not a new fad. It has been around for decades, therefore it would be a good idea to review it and see its progression over the years. There are two ways that the Ketogenic diet has evolved:

1. <u>Treatment of epileptic seizures</u>

The Ketogenic diet has been used in the past to treat children suffering from epilepsy. It has even been documented that fasting was used during the Middle Ages as a way to control seizures. The early 90s saw incidences of children being starved in order to control their seizures, but this was not a sustainable solution.

For this reason, studies were done to look for ways to mimic the effects of starvation while still providing food to the patient. The researchers found out that a diet high in fats, low in carbs, and with minimal protein was the best way to sustain starvation for as long as possible without harming the patient. Dr. Russell Wilder created the Ketogenic diet in 1921. He used it to treat epileptic children who had failed to improve after drug treatments.

The Ketogenic diet disappeared after the 1930s due to the introduction of modern medicines. In 1994, the Ketogenic diet made a comeback thanks to a two-year-old epileptic boy called Charlie Abraham. Neither brain surgery nor drugs could help Charlie, so his father did some research and discovered that the Ketogenic diet had been used successfully in the past to treat his son's condition.

Charlie's seizures were controllable only when he was on the Ketogenic diet. The Ketogenic diet is today widely accepted as a treatment for epilepsy in cases where conventional medicine fails to be effective.

2. **Treatment of obesity**
For over a hundred years, the Ketogenic diet was used to treat people suffering from excessive weight gain. The morbidly obese patients were normally starved of food, as it was believed that this measure

would lead to loss of weight. This form of fasting was reinforced by the fact that ketosis led to appetite suppression and improvement in wellbeing.

The problem with this type of therapy was that the body soon started eating its own protein, mainly muscle tissue. Apart from that, the weight that a person normally loses during fasting is mostly protein and water, not fat. If allowed to continue for too long, it can turn into potential health nightmare!

The 1970s saw numerous studies that revealed the impact of low-carb diets on people with obesity. The conclusion was that, theoretically, consuming a diet containing less than 50 grams of carbs every day would cause you to eat less food. It was around this time that the Dr. Atkins Diet was developed, and it advocated for a high fat, moderate protein, and low carb diet.

It is important to understand how the Ketogenic diet works as well as its history. There is a lot of information that is disseminated out there regarding this diet, so you have to ensure that the information you receive is accurate and credible. This chapter has covered the basics of what you need to know before you get started. In the next chapter, we shall look at the impact the Ketogenic diet has on transforming your body, as well as its many benefits.

Chapter 2: Impacts and Terms of the Ketogenic Diet

Most people have become used to consuming high-carb foods on a daily basis. This means that our bodies become accustomed to breaking down carbohydrates into two components: **glucose and glycogen.** The body does not normally produce a lot of enzymes for breakdown of fats since they are generally stored for future use. Whenever the body detects a reduction in glucose or glycogen levels, it increases the production of fat-burning enzymes.

The Ketogenic diet generally depletes your liver and muscles of their glycogen reserves. The ultimate result will be fatigue, lethargy, dizziness, and even headaches. These are all the effects of a reduction in electrolyte levels. How does this occur?

Carbohydrates are known to cause water retention in the body, especially within the muscles. When you start a Ketogenic diet, you drastically drop your carbohydrate intake, thus reducing the amount of water in the body. This is similar to a diuretic effect.

A reduction in water retention in the body causes loss of weight as well as the effects mentioned above.

The solution to this reduction in electrolyte levels is to increase the amount of water and sodium you consume. This is the best way to tackle the initial transition period of your ketosis.

In most cases, people who consume between twenty to forty grams of carbohydrates daily take a minimum of 14 days to experience ketosis. However, there are certain things you can do to essentially quicken the process. Firstly, you can reduce carbohydrate consumption to 15 grams per day. This will ensure that you get into the Ketogenic phase within one week. Another measure you can take is to exercise. Lifting weights and running sprints have been proven to reduce the adaptation time that your body needs to enter ketosis.

The initial days of the diet will be characterized by low energy and strength. However, once your **body adapts** to breaking down fats instead of glycogen and glucose, you will be surprised to discover that you have **more energy than ever before.**

Ketogenic Dieting Principles

In order to get the most out of your Ketogenic diet, you have to understand some of its basic principles and concepts. Most people who want to lose weight tend to focus primarily on bodyweight as the only measure of the effectiveness of a diet regimen. However, this is not a holistic perspective. Another factor has to be taken into account – the ratio of your body fat to your total body weight. This is also referred to as body composition.

Bodyweight versus Body fat

There is a huge difference between losing weight and losing fat. It is surprisingly simple and easy to lose weight within a very short time. If you go for three days without drinking any water, you are likely to lose up to five pounds of bodyweight. This may seem to be a great achievement, but remember, you haven't really lost anything. The moment you start drinking water, you begin to gain back the weight.

What you want to experience is fat loss. This means that you have to make sure that the weight you are losing is from fat reserves and not water or muscle wastage. Another important thing to remember is that as your fat levels reduce, your lean mass should remain constant or increase. However, most people tend to experience some loss of muscle mass as they cut fat from the body. The reason for this is usually a lack of exercise. That is why you are advised to always include exercise in your Ketogenic diet. It will ensure that as you lose weight from fat reduction, your body spares the protein in form of muscle mass.

Body Composition

This is another important factor that you need to keep your mind on. Yes, you may be losing weight, but what about your body fat to bodyweight ratio? Your bodyweight is generally split into two masses – fat and lean muscle. In order to calculate your body composition, you have to find your percentage body fat. This is done as follows:

Body fat % = Fat mass/Total bodyweight

The key thing to remember is that you should always aim to reduce body fat percentage by cutting the fat from your body. Alternatively, you can also reduce your body fat percentage by increasing muscle mass through exercise. The bottom line is that a combined approach consisting of the Ketogenic diet and exercise will give you the best chance of losing fat quickly while boosting your energy levels.

Chapter 3: Benefits of the Ketogenic Diet

The Ketogenic diet is one that should be embraced as a lifestyle. It provides you with many inherent benefits that other high-carb diets cannot. Even if you decide to achieve the state of ketosis for only a brief period of time, the health benefits you will experience will amaze you. Outlined below are some of the benefits that you will enjoy with a Ketogenic diet.

Benefits of the Ketogenic Diet

1. **It elevates your energy production.** Eating too many carbs tends to cause constant spikes and drops in energy levels. The Ketogenic diet eliminates this, thus allowing your body to have constantly high energy and focus levels.

2. **There is a reduction in levels of insulin.** This will allow your body to break down fats more efficiently, compared to a normal high-carb diet. There are also certain hormones that are released when insulin levels are low, for example, muscular growth hormones.

Remember, when muscles grow, you lose weight.

3. **A high fat and moderate protein diet keeps you fuller for longer.** You will notice that even when in ketosis, you will not experience the hunger pangs you used to endure when consuming a lot of carbohydrates.

4. **When in ketosis, your body becomes more efficient at generating fuel for its functions.** The problem with a high carb diet is that it makes the metabolic system sluggish and lazy. Ketosis forces the body to up its game!

5. The Ketogenic diet prevents your body from breaking down its own proteins for energy production in favor of ketones derived from fats. This is referred to as **"protein sparing."** This means that muscle tone will be preserved.

6. **When your body is in ketosis, it will trigger the excretion of excess ketone bodies via urination.** We discussed before about ketone bodies being derived from fats, so whenever you remove the surplus ketones

from your body, you are actually reducing your body fat percentage. This will ultimately reduce your bodyweight.

Chapter 4: Ketogenic Recipes

This chapter contains some delicious Ketogenic recipes that are also gluten-free. They have been categorized into breakfast, lunch, and dinner meals, as well as some snacks.

Breakfast Recipes

Western Omelet

Servings: 2
Prep Time: 10 minutes
Cook Time: 15 minutes
Nutrition: 72% fat
     25% protein
     3% carbs (5g of carbs per serving)

Ingredients:

- 6 eggs
- 2 tablespoons heavy whipping cream or sour cream

- salt and pepper
- 3½ oz. shredded cheese
- 2 oz. butter
- ½ yellow onion, finely chopped
- ½ green bell pepper, finely chopped
- 4¾ oz. ham, diced

Method:

1. Whisk eggs and cream(or sour cream instead) in a mixing bowl until they become **fluffy.** Add salt and pepper according to the taste.
2. Now add half of the shredded cheese and mix it well.
3. Put the butter in a frying pan and melt it on medium heat. Saute the diced ham, onion and peppers for a **few minutes.** Now add the egg mixture and fry it until the omelet becomes firm. Be mindful of not burning the edges. Take extra care.
4. Lower the heat after sometime. Sprinkle the rest of the cheese on top of the omelet and fold it.
5. Serve it hot. **Enjoy** the delicious and healthy omelet!

Tip!

Try it with a salad, a fresh green one. You can also use some sauce to make it a little spicy if you want to. Personal preference there. **Cheers!**

The Egg Muffins

Serving: 4
Prep Time: 5 minutes
Cook Time: 20 minutes
Nutrition: 72% fat
   26% protein
   2% carbs(2g of carbs per serving)

Ingredients:

- 6 eggs
- 1 – 2 scallions, finely chopped
- 4 – 8 thin slices of air dried chorizo or salami or cooked bacon
- 3½ oz. shredded cheese
- 1 tablespoon red pesto or green pesto (not necessary)
- Pepper and salt

Method:

1. First of all, preheat the oven to 350°F.
2. Chop the meat and the scallions.

3. Whisk the eggs together with pesto and seasoning. Now add the cheese and then stir.
4. Now place the batter in the form of muffins and then add bacon,salami or chorizo.
5. Now depending on the size of the muffin forms, bake them for 15-20 minutes.
6. Serve and **enjoy**.

Tip!

The best part about making these muffins is that **kids just love them**. So, they can be very handy for your kid's lunchbox. That lunchbox will definitely be **empty** after the school.

Salad Sandwiches

Servings: 4
Prep Time: 2 minutes
Cook Time: 0 minutes
Nutrition: 77% fat
    22% protein
    1% carbs(1g of carbs per serving)

Ingredients:

- 3 leaves of cosmopolitan lettuce or romaine hearts
- butter
- Cheese slices
- avocado
- Dried meat
- Tomato

Method:

1. Choose a very **crisp and firm** lettuce variety, preferably cosmopolitan lettuce or romaine.
2. Wash the lettuce thoroughly and use it as a base for the toppings.

Tip!

Play around with the toppings as per your choice but keep in mind the nutrient value also because changing the toppings will also change the nutrient value of the recipe. Tuna salad and egg salad can be good alternatives. Let the kids select their favorite toppings.

No Bread Breakfast Sandwich

Servings: 2
Prep Time: 5 minutes
Cook Time: 10 minutes
Nutrition: 72% fat
     27% protein
     1% carbs (0g carbs per serving)

Ingredients:

- 4 eggs
- 2 tablespoons butter
- 1 oz. ham
- 2 oz. cheddar cheese or provolone cheese or edam cheese, cut in thick slices
- salt and pepper
- a few drops of Tabasco or Worcestershire sauce

Method:

1. Fry the eggs on **medium heat** over easy. Add salt and pepper according to the taste.
2. Now for each sandwich, use the fried egg as a base. Now place the ham/cold cuts/pastrami on

each of the stack. Add cheese now. Now top off with a fried egg.

3. A few drops of Tabasco or Worcestershire sauce will add to the flavor.

4. Serve **hot!**

Tip!

Unsweetened mustard is a very good match with the ham. You can also skip the meat and go with green salad or avocado.

Iced Tea

Servings: 2
Prep Time: 10 minutes
Cook time: 2 hours

Ingredients:

- 2 cups cold water
- 1 tea bag
- 1 cup ice cubes
- Flavorings of your choice, such as sliced lemon or fresh mint

Method:

1. Take half of the cold water in a pitcher and add the tea and flavoring to it and put it in the refrigerator for **2 hours.**
2. Now take out the pitcher and remove the tea bag and flavoring. Replace it with new flavoring if you want.
3. Now add the ice cubes and the rest of the cold water to it and **serve.**

Tip!

You can try this with any kind of tea that you want. You can add lemon or a few leaves of mint to give it a flavor. There are lots of **creative and delicious ways** for it.

Mushroom Omelet

Serving: 1
Prep Time: 5 minutes
Cook Time: 10 minutes
Nutrition: 76% fat
    21% protein
    3% carbs (4g of carbs per serving)

Ingredients:

- 3 eggs
- 7/8 oz. butter, for frying
- 7/8 oz. shredded cheese
- 1/5 yellow onion
- 2 – 3 mushrooms
- Pepper and salt.

Method:

1. Crack the eggs and put them into a mixing bowl. Add a pinch of pepper and salt. Whisk the eggs with a spoon or fork until they become **smooth and frothy.**
2. Add spices and salt according to the taste.

43

3. Put butter in a frying pan and melt it. Once the butter is melted, pour in the egg mixture.
4. When the omelet begins to cook and get a little firm, but still has a little raw egg on top, sprinkle cheese, mushrooms and onion on top (totally optional).
5. Using a spatula, carefully ease around the edges of the omelet. And then fold it over. When it begins to turn golden brown underneath, remove the pan from the heat and slide the omelet on to a plate.

Tip!

Serve the omelet hot and crispy with some green salad with a **vinaigrette dressing**. So Yummy!

__Dairy Free Latte__

Servings: 2
Prep Time: 5 minutes
Cook Time: 0 minutes
Nutrition: 85% fat
    25% protein
    0% carbs(0g carbs per serving)

Ingredients:

- 2 eggs
- 2 tablespoons coconut oil
- 12/3 cups boiling water
- 1 pinch vanilla extract
- 1 teaspoon pumpkin pie spice or ground ginger

Method:

1. Take a blender and blend all the ingredients in it.
2. Drink and enjoy.

Tip!

You can replace the spices with one tablespoon of **cocoa or instant coffee**, if you want chocolate or plain latte. **Cheers!**

Keto Porridge

Servings: 1
Prep Time: 5 minutes
Cook Time: 5 minutes
Nutrition: 90% fat
     7% protein
     3% carbs(4g of carbs per serving)

Ingredients:

- 1 tablespoon chia seeds
- 1 tablespoon sesame seeds
- 1 egg
- 5⅓ tablespoons heavy whipping cream
- 1 pinch salt
- 1 oz. butter or coconut oil

Method:

1. Take all the ingredients and mix them in a bowl **except butter.** Let it sit for **2-3** minutes.
2. Take a small pan and melt butter or oil in it on medium heat.

3. Now pour the other ingredients and continue to stir until the porridge becomes firm. Do not let the porridge boil, let it simmer.
4. Serve it hot with melted butter.
5. **Enjoy!**

Coffee With Cream

Serving: 1
Prep Time: 5 minutes
Cook Time: 0 minutes
Nutrition: 93% fat
   4% protein
   3% carbs(2g carbs per serving)

Ingredients:

- ¾ cup coffee, brewed the way you like it
- 4 tablespoons heavy whipping cream

Method:

1. Make your coffee your own way, **the way you like it.**
2. Take a small saucepan and pour the cream into it and heat gently while stirring and until its frothy.
3. Now pour the warm cream in a cup and add coffee to it and stir.
4. Serve it as it is or with a handful of nuts or a little bit of cheese. Enjoy.

Tip!

Add a dark chocolate to your coffee with lots of cocoa solids. This way, when you finish your coffee you will have a **melted treat** for you. Cheers!

Coconut Porridge

Serving: 1
Prep Time: 0 minutes
Cook Time: 10 minutes
Nutrition: 87% fat
    10% protein
    3% carbs(4g of carbs per serving)

Ingredients:

- 1 oz. butter
- 1 egg
- 1 tablespoon coconut flour
- 1 pinch ground psyllium husk powder
- 4 tablespoons coconut cream
- 1 pinch salt

Method:

1. Take a **non stick saucepan** and mix all the ingredients in it over a low heat. **Stir constantly** until you achieve the desired texture.
2. Serve it with coconut milk or cream. A few fresh or frozen berries can be used as a topping.

3. Serve and enjoy.

Tip!

The leftover coconut milk can be reused, put some into your next smoothie. It will add a little fat to it and also thicken it up a bit.

Caprese Omelet

Servings: 2
Prep Time: 10 minutes
Cook Time: 10 minutes
Nutrition: 72% fat
    25% protein
    3% carbs(3g of carbs per serving)

Ingredients:

- 2 tablespoons olive oil
- 6 eggs
- 3½ oz. cherry tomatoes cut in halves or tomatoes cut in slices
- 1 tablespoon fresh basil or dried basil
- ⅓ lb fresh mozzarella cheese
- salt and pepper

Method:

1. Take a mixing bowl, crack the eggs into it and add the salt and pepper according to your taste. Use a fork to whisk until **fully combined.** Add basil to it and then stir.

2. Cut the tomatoes in halves or slice, whatever you like. Dice or slice the cheese.
3. Take a large frying pan and heat oil in it. Now fry the tomatoes for a **few minutes.**
4. Now take the egg batter and pour it on top of the tomatoes. Wait until the batter is slightly firm before adding the mozzarella cheese.
5. Now lower the heat and let the omelet set.
6. Serve immediately and **Enjoy!**

Cheese Omelet

Servings: 2
Prep Time: 4 minutes
Cook Time: 10 minutes
Nutrition: 78% fat
    20% protein
    2% carbs (4g of carbs per serving)

Ingredients:

- 6 eggs
- 3 oz. butter
- 7 oz. shredded cheddar cheese
- salt and pepper to taste

Method:

1. Whisk the eggs until they become **smooth and a little frothy.** Blend in half of the shredded cheddar. Pepper and Salt must be according to the taste.
2. Take the butter and melt it in a hot frying pan.
3. Now pour in the egg mixture and let it set for a few minutes.

4. Lower the heat slightly and continue cooking until the egg mixture is almost cooked through. Now add all the remaining cheese. Fold and serve immediately. **Enjoy!**

Tip!

You can also add chopped vegetables, herbs and even a side of salsa. Use olive oil or coconut oil to cook your omelet for a different flavor.

Raspberry Protein Pancakes

This Ketogenic breakfast dish contains 275 calories in total – 55 grams of fat, 36 grams of proteins, 29 grams of carbohydrates, and 9 grams of fiber.

Ingredients:

- ¼ cup egg whites
- 2 Tbsp Greek yogurt
- 1 scoop protein powder
- ¾ cup frozen raspberries
- 1 Tbsp Cinnamon
- ½ a banana
- 2 Tbsp almond milk
- 1 Tbsp Chia seeds

Method:

1. Grind the Chia seeds.
2. Mash the banana
3. Take a bowl and put in all the ingredients. Leave the raspberries out. Mix thoroughly.
4. After mixing the ingredients well, toss in the raspberries and stir.

5. Sprinkle some Olive oil onto a pan. Pour the mixture into the pan and cook over medium heat until the edges of the pancakes turn brown, then flip.
6. Check to make sure that the middle part of the pancake is well cooked.
7. Serve the meal with the **Greek yogurt.**

The Perfect Bacon and Scrambled Eggs

This delicious Ketogenic breakfast contains 318 calories in total – 26.3 grams of fat, 17.4 grams protein, and 1.8 grams carbohydrates.

Ingredients:

- 3 large eggs
- 1 Tbsp unsalted butter
- Coarse salt
- Ground pepper

Method:

1. Break the eggs into a medium-sized bowl.
2. Take a medium nonstick skillet and place it over low heat. Place the butter in the skillet and allow it to melt.
3. Take a **heatproof spatula** and gently pull the eggs towards the center of the skillet. Cook the eggs for about **2 to 3 minutes.**
4. Add pepper and salt to taste.
5. Serve hot.

Lunch Recipe

Ground Beef Stir Fry

This Ketogenic dish contains 307 calories – 18 grams of fat, 29 grams of protein, and 7 grams of carbohydrates. It serves up to 3 people.

Ingredients:

- 10 ½ oz ground beef
- 2 leaves kale
- 1 Tbsp coconut oil
- ½ cup broccoli
- 5 brown mushrooms
- ½ medium Spanish onions
- 1 Tbsp Cayenne pepper
- ½ medium red peppers
- 1 Tbsp Chinese Five Spices

Method:

1. Chop the red pepper, onions, kales, and broccoli into pieces, and then slice the mushrooms.

2. Pour the coconut oil into a large skillet and cook the onions for **one minute** with medium-high heat.

3. Toss in the chopped vegetables and cook them for another **two minutes.** Keep stirring throughout.

4. Add the spices and ground beef into the skillet. Reduce the heat to medium and cook for about **two minutes.**

5. Place a lid over the skillet and cook for about **10 more minutes,** until the beef becomes brown.

Cocoa Butter Keto Blondies

Servings: 20 blondies
Prep time: 15 minutes
Cook time: 30 minutes
Nutrition: 70% fat
     20% protein
     10% carbs

Ingredients:

- 1/4 cup almond flour
- 2 tablespoon coconut flour
- 1/4 teaspoon baking soda
- 1/4 teaspoon salt
- 6 tablespoon cocoa butter
- 4 tablespoon butter unsalted
- 2 large eggs
- 1/2 cup erythritol
- 1 teaspoon vanilla extract
- 2 tablespoon coconut cream
- 1/2 oz. dark chocolate chopped
- 2 tablespoon walnuts or any nuts or chia (optional)

Method:

1. Firstly preheat the oven to **320°F.** Now line a **baking pan (8*9 inch)** with some parchment paper. Measure out all the ingredients now.

2. Now take a microwave safe bowl and cut the butter and cocoa butter into it. Let them melt in the microwave for **90 seconds.** Now take the mixture out and stir the mixture and make sure there are no lumps left. If required, microwave for another **60 seconds** or so. Let it cool now.

3. Take a **hand electric mixer** and mix the eggs, erythritol, and vanilla extract. Now add the coconut cream and mix it again.

4. Now take the cooled butter and pour it into it. Mix it until the mixture gets denser and creamy.

5. Now **sieve and mix** the two flours, baking soda and salt. Add the flour mixture to the cream and combine it well with a rubber spatula.

6. Add the chopped chocolate and stir it well again.

7. Now take the mixture and put it into a baking pan and spread it out evenly, using a **spatula.**

8. Bake it for **30 minutes** in the oven. Make sure that the blondies are a little bit fudgy in the middle. Do not over bake them.

9. When the baking is complete, take out the whole batch from the pan together with the parchment paper and then let it cool. Cut it into **20 pieces** (size and number is your choice) of equal size when its cooled.

10. Serve and **Enjoy!**

Dinner Recipe

Ketogenic Reuben Casserole

This dinner recipe contains 360 calories per serving – 25 grams of fat, 14 grams of protein, 5 grams of carbohydrates, and 2 grams of fiber.

Ingredients:

- 2 cups shredded Swiss cheese
- 8 oz. cream cheese
- ½ pound corned beef
- ½ cup mayonnaise
- 2 Tbsp pickle brine
- 1 can of drained sauerkraut
- ½ cup low-sugar ketchup
- ½ tsp Caraway seeds

Method:

1. Heat the oven to about **662** degrees Fahrenheit.
2. Slice the corned beef into chunks.

3. Put the mayonnaise, ketchup, and cream cheese in a saucepan. Heat the mixture until it melts.
4. Add the beef chunks into the saucepan. Toss in **1 ½ cups** of the Swiss cheese and one can of drained sauerkraut. Stir well.
5. Take the saucepan off the heat and sprinkle the pickle brine.
6. Get a greased dish and pour the mix into it. Add the **½ cup** of shredded Swiss cheese that was left over. Top it off with the Caraway seeds.
7. Put the dish in the preheated oven for about **20 minutes.** Once the mixture begins to bubble and the cheese melts, remove it from the oven.

Coconut Lime Skirt Steak

Servings: 2
Prep Time: 10 minutes
Cook Time: 40 minutes

Ingredients:

- 1/2 cup coconut oil, melted
- zest of one lime
- 2 tablespoon freshly squeezed lime juice from one lime
- 1 tablespoon minced garlic
- 1 teaspoon grated fresh ginger (I used the fresh stuff in the tube)
- 1 teaspoon red pepper flakes
- 3/4 tsp sea salt
- 2lb grass fed skirt steak (you can cut it into sections)

Method:

1. Combine the coconut oil with lime juice and zest, garlic, ginger, red pepper flakes and salt in a large bowl. **Mix them properly.**

2. Now add the steak toss/rub with marinade.(After you are done, the coconut oil will harden)
3. Now for about almost **20 minutes,** let the meat marinate at room temperature. It is **very important** to marinate the meat.
4. Now take your steak to a large skillet set, which is set over medium high heat. If the steak does not fit then cut it into half. Cut the steak **against the grain.** Some of your marinade can still be stuck to the bowl, spoon it out in to the pan and cook it with the steak.
5. Now cook the steak on each side for about **5 minutes.** Skirt steaks does not take much time to cook.
6. Now slice it and **serve!**

Cauliflower Soup

Servings: 4
Prep Time: 5 minutes
Cook Time: 15 minutes
Nutrition: 90% fat
     7% protein
     3% carbs(5g of carbs per serving)

Ingredients:

- 3¾ cups chicken stock or vegetable stock
- 1 lb cauliflower
- 7¾ oz. cream cheese
- 1 tbsp Dijon mustard
- 4 oz. butter
- Pepper and Salt
- 7 oz. panchetta or bacon, diced
- 1 tbsp butter, for frying
- 1 tsp paprika powder or smoked chili powder
- 3½ oz. pecan nuts

Method:

1. The first step is to trim the cauliflower and cut it into small florets. Cut them small for the soup to be ready faster.

2. Now take a handful of cauliflower(fresh) and chop it into tiny bits.
3. Now sauté the chopped cauliflower and pancetta in the butter until they become crispy.
4. Add the paprika powder and the nuts towards the end and then set aside the mixture and save the fat.
5. Meanwhile, take the cauliflower florets and **boil them** in the stock until they become **soft**. Now add cream cheese, butter and mustard.
6. Mix it with a hand blender. The **more you blend,** the **creamier the soup** will be. Add salt and pepper according to your taste.
7. Serve in bowls, and **top it** with panchetta and cauliflower crumbles in the end.
8. **Enjoy!**

Butter Coffee Rubbed Tri Tip Steak

Servings: 2
Prep Time: 10 minutes
Cook Time: 35 minutes
Nutrition: 75% fat
    21% protein
    4% carbs(4g of carbs per serving)

Ingredients:

- 2 Tri-tip steaks (of course the other cuts of beef would work too)
- 1 teaspoon course ground black pepper
- 1/2 tablespoon sea salt
- 1 package of Coffee Blocks
- 1/2 tablespoon garlic powder
- 2 tablespoon olive oil

Method:

1. Take the meat and let it sit at room temperature for about **15-20 minutes.** Take a mallet and pound the meat to tenderize(optional).

2. Combine all the ingredients in a bowl except steak.
3. Now rub the mixture all over steaks (top, bottom and sides).
4. On a **medium high heat**, heat a skillet with the olive oil.
5. Now add steaks to skillet and cook for **5** minutes on one side. It will also keep the coffee from **burning.**
6. Now flip it and cook on the other side for another **5** minutes.
7. Remove the pan and let it sit there in its own juices. Let it reabsorb them. **Yummy!**
8. Now cut the steak into slices against the grain and then enjoy your **Delicious Piece of Art.**

Tip!

This would also be very delicious with skirt steak also. Cook skirt steak on high because it needs to be cooked shorter and hotter.

Keto Swedish Meatballs

Servings: 4
Prep Time: 20 minutes
Cook Time: 2 hour 20 minutes

Ingredients:

- 2 lbs ground meatloaf blend (or 1 lb ground beef and 1lb ground pork is fine)
- 1 cup shredded mild Cheddar cheese
- 1 large egg
- 1 tbsp water
- 1/4 cup diced onions
- 1/2 tsp ground nutmeg
- 1/4 tsp allspice
- 4 tbsp salted butter
- 1.5 cups chicken broth
- 1.5 cups heavy (whipping) cream
- 1 tbsp Dijon mustard
- 1 tbsp Worcestershire sauce

Method:

1. Preheat the oven to **400°F** and also preheat a slow cooker to low.
2. Now line a big baking pan with parchment paper.
3. Now **combine** ground meat with cheddar cheese, egg, onion, water, allspice and nutmeg in a big bowl.
4. Now roll the mixture into **1.5-2 inch** meatballs and put them on the lined baking pan. Make around **20-25 meatballs.** You might need 2 baking pans depending on the size of your baking pan.
5. Now keep baking for about **20 minutes.**
6. Meanwhile, heat the butter, chicken broth and heavy cream over medium heat in a small skillet.
7. Now it will begin to simmer. Once it starts simmering, reduce the heat to low and let it simmer for about **20 minutes** until it reduces to half. Stir frequently towards the end.
8. Now stir in the Worcestershire sauce and mustard.
9. Now its time to pour the sauce into the slow cooker. Add the meatballs whenever they are ready.
10. Now cook on the low heat for about **2 hours.** It will give the meatballs the time to marinate.
11. Keep stirring after **every half hour,** covering all the meatballs.

Tip!

Do not cook in the slow cooker for more than 2 hours. Cooking more than 2 hours can cause the **sauce to separate.**

*This recipe is not for you if you are a beginner at cooking. This is more sort of an **advanced recipe** and requires a little bit of experience in cooking.

Dessert Recipe

Low Carb Pie Crust

This is a delectable dessert recipe that is used to make miniature tart shells.

Ingredients:

- 2 large eggs
- 4 Tbsp melted butter
- 2 cups almond flour
- 1 tsp salt

Method:

1. Preheat the oven to **662** degrees Fahrenheit.
2. Place the almond flour and melted butter into a bowl and mix them well.
3. Add the eggs and salt as you keep mixing. Ideally, the dough is supposed to pull toward the middle of the bowl and form a ball. If not, add some more flour.

4. Take the ball of dough and put it on parchment paper. Cover it with a sheet of parchment paper.
5. Take a rolling pin and make ¼" thick rectangular shapes. Cut circles in the dough using a biscuit cutter.
6. Line a cupcake pan with cupcake paper and place the dough circles on the pan. Put the pan in the preheated oven and heat until the edges turn golden.
7. **Serve and enjoy!**

Snack Recipe

Kale and Bacon Chips

As a Ketogenic snack, this dish serves up about 62 calories for every cup of kale used. It contains 6 grams of fat, 1 gram of protein, and 1 gram of carbohydrates.

Ingredients:

- 5 cups kale leaves
- 2 Tbsp butter
- ½ cup bacon grease
- 2 tsp salt

Method:

1. Preheat the oven to **662** degrees Fahrenheit.
2. Remove the stems from the kale leaves and chop the leaves into small pieces. Use a salad spinner to wash and dry them.
3. Place the bacon grease and butter in a pan and heat the mixture till it melts. Add the salt and stir.

4. Put all the kale pieces inside a Ziploc bag and pour the bacon grease-butter mixture into the bag. Without sealing the bag, shake the bag until all the leaves have been coated with the mixture. Use your hands to coat the leaves thoroughly.

5. Take a cookie sheet and line it using parchment paper. Place the kales on the sheet.

6. Put the kales in the oven and heat until **brown and crispy.** The smaller bits of kale tend to cook faster so it is advisable to heat the larger and smaller pieces on separate cookie sheets.

Chapter 5: Basic Principles

- **Stick with the basic keto ratio: 61-75%** of calories from the fat, **14-30%** calories from the protein and **6-10%** calories from the net carbs.
- Start slowly. Get the daily net carbs (total carbs without fiber) down to at least less than **50** grams, preferably **20-30** grams. Increase slowly to find the optimal carbs intake for you. Most of the people are able to stay in ketosis at **20-30** grams of net carbs per day.
- Your protein intake should be **moderate**. Try to use your body fat percentage to get the best estimate for your optimal protein intake (**0.6 to 1** grams per pound of lean body mass or **1.3 to 2.2** grams per kg of lean body mass).
- You should try to increase the proportion of the calories that come from healthy fats (saturated, omega 3s, monounsaturated etc.)
- If the net carbs limit is very low (20 grams and below) then try to avoid eating fruit and low-carb treats.
- Eat whenever you are hungry, does not matter if it is a meal a day. Do not let others tell you what you should eat or how often you should eat.

- You do not have to deliberately **limit the quantities** of food that you are consuming, but you should definitely stop eating when ever you feel full, even if the plate is not empty, just save it for later.

- Do not count your calorie intake, just listen to what your body needs and demands. Ketogenic diet and low-carb diets have a natural appetite control effect and you will automatically eat less. You should keep an eye on your calorie intake only if you reach a weight loss plateau.

- Water is really important in this diet. Increase the intake of water that you have now. You must be drinking 2-3 liters of water everyday.

- Try to eat **real foods** like eggs, meat and non-starchy veggies. This might be contrary to what we have been told for decades but these are very good for you!

- If you want to **snack,** go for healthy foods high in fat (foods containing coconut oil, avocados, macadamia nuts, etc.)

- Try to include some healthy foods like fermented foods, bone broth and offal in your day to day diet.

- Do not be afraid of the **saturated fat** and you can use it for cooking (coconut oil, butter, lard, tallow, ghee, palm oil - organic from sustainable agriculture). No problem in this.

- Always use **unsaturated fats for salads** (olive oil, nut oils, sesame oil, flaxseed oil, avocado oil - organic, extra virgin). Some of them can be used for light cooking.
- Just **avoid** all of the following things:
  - Processed vegetable oils
  - Margarine
  - Hydrogenated oils
  - Partially hydrogenated oils
  - Corn oil
  - Canola oil
  - Soybean oil
  - Grapeseed oil
  - Trans fat

- Try to eat **raw dairy** (none in case of allergies). And look for raw, organic and grass-fed dairy. Just avoid milk (high in carbs) or use small amounts of unpasteurized full-fat milk.
- If you want to eat nuts, try to **soak and dehydrate** them first.
- Never trust the products labeled as "Low Carb". You can not afford to put your health as risk. Labeled products can be dangerous in Ketogenic Diet. Natural foods must always be the priority. Focus on the foods that are naturally low in carbohydrates. Make sure you always opt for real and unprocessed food.

- Labeled products are always deceptive, they are often higher in carbs than they claim. So consuming these kind of products can harm your plans. Labeled products often contain artificial additives which are not allowed in the keto diet. Aspartame (an artificial sweetener) which is present in the diet soda is not at all healthy and has shown many adverse effects on our health. The big companies have financial interests and they deceive the customer in every possible way. So always go for the natural and unprocessed food and do not fall in to the trap of labeled products.

Beware of the hidden carbs and the unhealthy ingredients

- Always read the labels and try to avoid hidden carbs, unnecessary additives, colourings, preservatives or artificial sweeteners. These are found even in chewing gums and mints. They can **trigger cravings** for sugar and they are also not good for health. If you want use sweeteners, go for those with no effect on blood sugar.
- Just avoid everything labeled as **"low-fat"** or **"fat-free",** as it usually has artificial additives and extra carbs. These type of foods also have no sating effect and you will feel hungry soon after you have eaten it.
- Try to avoid the products which are labeled **"low-carb"** or **"great for low-carb diets"**. It has been shown that most of these commercially available products are not healthy. They are also not low carb. They are introduced in the market for financial purposes only. Try to avoid them or choose the best ones only.

- **Medicines:** Cough syrups and drops contain sugar. So try to find sugar-free replacements.

Increase the intake of Electrolyte

We always focus on the **macro-nutrients** (fat, carbs and protein) but neglect the **micro-nutrients** (vitamins and minerals). This is not a good habit. They are equally important and our body constantly requires their intake.

In a low carb diet, there is a deficiency of electrolytes, especially in very low-carb diets such as below 20 g net carbs

Here are a few tips to get your daily electrolytes:

1. **Potassium:** To increase the intake of potassium eat avocados, mushrooms, fatty fishes such as salmon and add potassium chloride to your regular salt (or mix ½ tsp in one litre of water and drink it throughout the day). Be very careful with potassium supplements, do not exceed the recommended daily intake. Never!
2. **Magnesium:** To increase the intake of magnesium one should eat a handful of nuts every day and take magnesium supplement. If you are eating less than 20-25 grams of net carbs

daily then it will be very difficult for you to get to your daily targets.

3. **Sodium:** Do not be afraid to use salt and drink bone broth or use it in your everyday cooking.

Always plan your diet in advance and avoid the accidents.

If you want to save your money as well as your time then you will need to plan your diet in advance. And if you are new to this type of diet and lifestyle then it becomes more important for you. Here are some tips before you get started:

- Just get rid of everything that is not allowed on the diet (flour, sugar and sugary snacks, bread, processed foods, etc.) to avoid any kind of temptation. Trust me, if it is in your house, you will likely crave it. This is the only way to avoid the unnecessary **"fridge accidents".** These accidents may ruin all your efforts.
- Just make sure that some keto friendly food is always available to you like avocado, meat, nuts, cheese, some non starchy veggies or some home made protein bars. Foods that are rich in protein

are very sating and they will always help you fight you **hunger cravings.**

- Do you have sugar cravings? Well if you do then I have a **solution** for it. Just drink a glass of water (sparkling or still) with fresh lime or lemon juice and 4-5 drops of stevia. You can also drink some tea or coffee with cream.

- Do not forget to make a list for your weekly shopping. This is very important. Plan your week and then make a list of things you will require to cook your recipes. Not having the right ingredients when you are planning to cook something is always a pain in the butt so be prepared and plan everything and make a list and then go shopping.

- We all want to save some time and also save some money. For this have hard boiled eggs and cooked meat ready to be used in salad or for a quick snack. Meat (slow cooked) like this one could be used in a lot of different ways (in omelet or on top or lettuce and other veggies). Meats which are suitable for slow cooking are cheaper and they can be cooked in advance. Use slow cooker for this or you can simply cook it in the oven on low-medium covered with a lid.

Chapter 6: Misconceptions and Mistakes to Avoid

If you do your own research, you will discover that there is a lot of **negative information** about the Ketogenic diet being propagated out there. The opposition to this diet is severe, yet the Ketogenic diet is not something new or unhealthy. What is unhealthy and unnatural is the way modern society prepares and eats its foods.

If you plan on going on a Ketogenic diet, you will have to know how to sift out the noise and get to the core of the truth. That is why you have picked up this book. Getting factual information about ketosis will help you avoid some of the many mistakes that people fall into, thinking they are heading in the right direction.

The mistakes people make are usually either dietary mistakes or lifestyle mistakes. You may have been **misinformed about how the diet works,** and even though you are using it, you are not doing so as effectively as possible. It is also possible that though you are committed to the Ketogenic diet, there are some old bad habits that you have refused to let go.

Enjoying the full benefits of the Ketogenic diet may require you to change your behavior or lifestyle.

Here are **8 of the most common mistakes** that most people make when on the Ketogenic diet and some of the ways to resolve them:

Inadequate consumption of water, vitamins, and minerals

When in ketosis, never make the mistake of eating insufficient mineral salts, vitamins, or drinking insufficient water. Salt is very important in the Ketogenic diet. Most people tend to view salt as an enemy, but it is still critical to get about two teaspoons of salt every day. Drinking enough water will help you stay hydrated and avoid feelings of fatigue and nausea. Ketosis tends to cause a lot of salts and water to be excreted from the kidneys via urination, so make sure that you are getting enough of your minerals. If you live in an area that is very hot, drink extra water than usual.

Vitamins that you need to load up on include vitamin D. Consume foods such as beef broth or take supplements to boost your salt, potassium, and magnesium intake.

Eating processed Ketogenic food

Do not go to the supermarket and buy a range of processed Keto foods wrapped in packaging. The Ketogenic diet works best when you consume real whole foods. This is the best way to avoid all those hidden sugars and starches that manufacturers tend to sneak into their products. Not only will these cause you to gain weight, they can also negatively impact your general health.

If you can, always try to cook your own meals. If this is not possible, always make sure that you ask whoever cooked the food the ingredients that went into it. If it is a restaurant, check the online menu before you go out. Go for safe foods like salads, broiled or roasted dishes.

If you plan on making the Ketogenic diet a long-term lifestyle, then the best advice is to simply learn how to cook. It may seem time-consuming, but it is well worth it.

Eating too many wrong fats

The Ketogenic diet recommends the consumption of high quantities of fats. However, not all fats are created equal. It is a big mistake to assume that any kind of fat will work for this diet.

Some of the types of fats to avoid include seeds and vegetable oils; especially the ones that come packed in plastic containers. These fats and oils will make you gain weight and damage your health in the long run. Artificial trans fats and partially hydrogenated oils should also be avoided. These are usually found in margarine, cookies, French fries, and many fried foods. The effects of consuming these fats include diabetes, inflammation, and heart disease.

Make sure you always check labels before buying anything. The good kind of fats that you need to be eating can be found in fish, meat, chicken, avocados, walnuts, Olive oil, butter, almonds, Chia seeds, coconut oil, cheese, and many others.

Consuming insufficient amounts of fat

The Ketogenic diet is known to be a high-fat diet, so why would you compromise its effectiveness by not consuming enough dietary fat? This is one mistake that can have the biggest impact on the success of your weight loss goals. The truth is that we have all grown up being told that fat is bad and therefore we should stay away from it. However, you knew from the beginning what the Ketogenic diet was all about. Not eating enough dietary fat is a huge mistake.

People who struggle with weight issues tend to think that fats are the problem, but the truth is that carbs and sugary foods are the real enemy. Take a good look at the kinds of food you eat every meal and you will see a clear imbalance towards excess carbs, especially processed carbohydrates.

Do not be afraid of consuming a lot of **GOOD** dietary fat. In fact, **80%** of your macro nutrient intake should be fats.

Eating too much protein

The Ketogenic diet calls for consumption of moderate amounts of protein. This is because the body cannot make all the amino acids by itself and therefore the diet must compensate for this. Some people tend to consume too much protein than is required for a Ketogenic diet. What is the problem with this kind of scenario?

When you eat a large meal comprising of proteins, more than half of it is turned into glucose. Remember that you are aiming to induce ketosis in your body, so ideally you want your body to break down fat for energy. Eating too much protein hinders this because the body will start to rely on proteins as an energy source rather than fat. You may be surprised to discover that you are on the

Ketogenic diet for a long while but aren't experiencing any meaningful weight loss. Furthermore, you will be in a constant cycle of reduced energy levels as your blood sugar rises and drops repeatedly.

It is advisable for you to consume not more than **1.7 g** of protein for every kilogram of your body weight. For a person who is consistently working out, try to increase protein intake to about **2 grams** per kilogram of body weight.

<u>Not getting enough exercise</u>

One misconception that people have against the Ketogenic diet is that you will be so weak and tired from the ketosis that you won't be able to exercise. This is simply not true. A lot of people have discovered that they are actually able to work out even when on this kind of diet.

Let's face it. Exercising comes with **numerous benefits.** You are trying to lose weight by reducing the fatty tissue in your body. You are also trying to generate more energy for yourself. Exercise can help you do both these things and much more.

There are two things you need to keep in mind, however. The first is that the initial weeks of the

Ketogenic diet will be very difficult as your body adapts to the new diet system. You will feel weak and somewhat unable to engage in moderate exercise. This is **OK**. Just wait for your body to adapt before you start exercising.

The second thing is that you should adopt some kind of weight training exercises as part of your routine. Cardio and aerobics are great, but lifting weights (keep them light if weight training isn't your thing) will build muscle, and we know that muscle boosts your metabolic rate. A higher metabolic rate will help you cut fat faster.

Skipping your adaptation period

If you are coming from a diet that is high in carbs and now want to switch to a high-fat low-carb diet, you are going to need an adaptation period. Some people make the mistake of jumping right in without gradually easing themselves into the new diet. The result is intense side effects that may make you quit the diet in the initial stages.

It has been noted that skipping the adaptation period may cause intense urges to clear out your bowels. You don't want this to happen when you are stuck in traffic somewhere or are in a meeting. Some people tend to think that there is something wrong with the diet because of this, or that their bodies are rebelling against the diet, but this is not true. The body may be versatile, but it needs time to adapt.

It is recommended that you ease into the Ketogenic diet by slowly lowering your carb intake and increasing your fat consumption over the same period of time. Your body needs to get used to burning fat rather than glucose to produce energy. If you feel hungry during this period, snack on some Ketogenic snacks like nuts, flax crackers, or almond butter. They will help fill you up, and the urge to snack will dissipate once your body finally adapts.

Lack of commitment and goal-setting

If you are going to make the Ketogenic diet work for you, **it is imperative that you stay committed to the cause**. Most people find it hard to maintain a Ketogenic diet successfully because they do not set clear and explicit goals of what they really want to achieve. This is why it becomes harder to stay committed in the long run.

Get a notebook or journal and write down how much weight you plan to lose, how much macro nutrients you will be consuming every day and the time frames for doing so. The success or failure of your goals hinges on how detailed and specific you are.

You also need to get rid of anything from your old carb-filled lifestyle. Clear out your house and give away those foods that do not align with your new **Ketogenic lifestyle.**

Conclusion

Thank you again for **purchasing this book!**

I hope this book was able to help you to appreciate the amazing ways that the Ketogenic diet can help you improve your overall health. You will be able to reduce your body fat levels while getting an incredible boost in everyday energy.

The next step is to take the necessary action and put into practice what you have learnt. Don't forget to consult your doctor before you start any kind of diet, especially if you have some underlying condition. All in all, I hope you enjoyed the book!

Finally, if you enjoyed this book, then I'd like to ask you for a favor, would you be kind enough to leave a review for this book on Amazon? It'd be greatly appreciated!

Click here to leave a review for this book on Amazon!

Ketogenic Diet

75+ Delicious Ketogenic Recipes for a healthy lifestyle.

Introduction

I would like to thank you for purchasing this book.

This book contains all the information that you will need to know about the ketogenic diet. The proven steps and strategies included herein will help you revolutionize your diet and your health in turn. In this book, you will find information about losing fat and improving your energy levels. If you have ever tried other forms of diets, and have found it extremely difficult to shed those extra kilos or even boost your energy levels, then this is the best diet for you.

Do you want to lose weight? Perhaps the word "diet" makes you anxious and nervous. Wouldn't it be nice if you could lose weight without having to stop eating? You might be thinking that this sounds absolutely ridiculous. No, your source of nutrition won't be restricted to just fruits and vegetables. Yes, you read it right. You will lose weight by making a simple change in your daily diet plan. The ketogenic diet is the perfect diet for those who want to lose weight without having to eat measly meals.

So, what exactly is the ketogenic diet? To put it simply, this is a diet where a person will need to consume a high amount of fats and low or no carbs. On this diet, 90% of your calorie requirement is fulfilled by fats, and the rest by proteins and carbs. This is a high fat and low carbohydrate based diet.

Our body makes use of carbohydrates for providing us with energy. Carbohydrates are broken down into glucose, the main source of energy. In a ketogenic diet, there is a shift in the basic source of energy in the body. From burning carbs for generating energy, the body will start burning fats. When the body starts making use of fats for providing energy, the liver starts secreting keto substances. The process of shifting from sugars to fats for producing energy is referred to as ketosis. This is where the diet gets its name.

A ketogenic diet encourages you to eat your fill of foods that you are allowed to eat. All the food items that are keto approved are rich in good fats. No processed carbs or sugars are allowed. If anything looks like it was produced in a factory, stay away from it. Instead of reaching over for a helping of mashed potatoes or pasta, have some grilled fatty meat instead. The number of calories you consume while on this diet will reduce, even though you are consuming fatty food.

During the initial phase of the ketogenic diet, you might feel a little low on energy. This is bound to happen since your body is just getting acclimatized to changing its basic source of fuel. Once your body gets used to burning fats for providing energy, you will start feeling energized and refreshed. You can work out like you used to. You needn't compromise on any physical activity that you used to be engaged in. in fact, if you want to lose weight quickly, it would be advisable that you start exercising or engaging in any physical activity.

The recipes that have been provided in this book are ketogenic diet friendly. These recipes are not only easy to cook but taste wonderful too. All that you will need to do is get the necessary ingredients and keep them on hand. If you plan ahead and pre-decide your meals, following the keto diet won't be difficult. It would be quite simple. You will need to stay strong and resist temptation. Be patient and you will definitely notice positive results in no time. Also, this diet helps you in losing fat from the abdominal region.

So, why don't we get started without any further ado?

Chapter 1: Ketogenic Breakfast Recipes

Berry Chocolate Shake

Servings: 2
Prep time: 5 minutes
Cook time: NA

Ingredients:
- 2 cups almond milk
- 1/2 cup blueberries / blackberries / strawberries / raspberries
- 1/4 cup cocoa powder
- Stevia drops to taste
- 1/2 teaspoon xanthan gum
- 2 tablespoons MCT oil
- Few ice cubes

Method:
1. Blend together all the ingredients until smooth.
2. Pour into tall glasses and serve.

Deviled Eggs

Servings: 6
Prep time: 10 minutes
Cook time: 15 minutes

Ingredients:
- 12 large eggs
- 1/2 cup mayonnaise
- ¼ cup finely minced white onion
- 1/2 teaspoon ground mustard
- 2 tablespoons of melted butter
- ½ teaspoon white pepper
- 1 teaspoon salt

Method:
1. Pour in cold water into a large pot and place the eggs in it.
2. Bring it to a boil and cook it for ten minutes.
3. Drain out the hot water. Pour in some more cold water over the eggs.
4. Remove the eggs from the water and peel off the shells.
5. Cut the eggs into halves. Remove the yellow yolks and keep it aside.
6. Finely crumble the cooked yolks. Add the remaining ingredients to the yolk and mix well.
7. Fill the white cavities of the egg with the yolk

mixture. Serve immediately.

Baked Bacon and eggs

Servings: 2
Prep time: 10 minutes
Cook time: 15 minutes

Ingredients:
- 4 large eggs
- 8 slices of cooked bacon, crumbled finely
- 1 cup cheddar cheese, finely grated
- 2 tablespoons butter
- 1 cup heavy cream, heated
- Salt
- Pepper

Method:
1. Pre heat the oven to 350 degrees F.
2. Take four ceramic ramekins and butter the insides of it.
3. Crack the eggs and pour one into each ramekin.
4. Add ¼ cup of cheddar cheese and ¼ cup of the lukewarm cream over the egg in a ramekin. Repeat the procedure with the other three ramekins.
5. Season the mixture well with the salt and pepper.
6. Place the ramekins in the oven and bake the mixture for around fifteen minutes until the egg whites are cooked and the cheese melts.
7. Sprinkle the finely crumbled bacon over the eggs and serve.

Matcha Smoothie Bowl

Servings: 2
Prep time: 5 minutes
Cook time: NA

Ingredients:

- 2 tablespoons goji berries
- 2 teaspoons matcha powder
- 2 tablespoons cacao nibs
- 2 tablespoons chia seeds
- 2 tablespoons coconut flakes
- 2 tablespoons chia seeds
- 2 cups coconut yogurt or full fat Greek yogurt
- 2 scoops greens powder (optional)

Method:

1. Add matcha powder, greens powder if using and yogurt to a blender and blend until smooth.
2. Pour into 2 individual bowls. Add rest of the ingredients to it.
3. Stir, chill for a while and serve.

Strawberry Lemon Smoothie

Servings: 1
Prep time: 5 minutes
Cook time: NA
Ingredients

- 1 cup water
- 2 tablespoons of apple cider vinegar
- 3 cups citrus juice
- 1 lemon
- 1/2 teaspoon ginger powder
- 6 strawberries

Method:

1. Add a cup of water, apple cider vinegar, ginger powder, strawberry and 3 cups of citrus juice to the blender.
2. Cut the lemon into halves and squeeze the juice into the mixture.
3. Blend the ingredients for a couple of minutes until the ingredients are mixed into a smooth mixture.
4. Serve chilled!

Chocolate Raspberry Protein Shake

Servings: 1
Prep time: 2 minutes
Cook time: NA

Ingredients
- 8 ounces almond milk (unsweetened)
- 2 ounces heavy cream
- 1 scoop Chocolate Whey Isolate Powder
- ½ tbsp. Sugar free raspberry syrup
- ½ cup crushed ice (you could add more or less as per your liking)

Method
1. Put all the ingredients in the blender and mix well. You have to ensure that the mixture is smooth.

Zucchini and Carrot Pancakes

Servings: 2-3
Prep time: 10 minutes
Cook time: 3-5 minutes

Ingredients
- 1 shredded carrot
- 1 shredded zucchini
- 1 cup almond flour
- 2 eggs
- 2 tbsp. low fat butter (unsalted)
- 1 tsp. dried basil
- 1 tsp. dried parsley
- Salt and pepper

Method
1. Take a clean and dry mixing bowl and transfer the almond flour, basil and shredded vegetables to it. Mix until the vegetables are coated with the flour.
2. Now continue mixing and add the salt, pepper and parsley to the bowl. Taste the batter to season it to your liking.
3. Break the eggs into the bowl and make sure the shell does not fall in. Whisk the ingredients using a blender. Obtain a smooth and creamy batter.
4. Make as many patties as you can from the batter that you have just prepared.
5. Take a saucepan and place it on a medium flame.

Add half a tsp. of butter to the pan. Once the butter has melted, cook the patties in it well until they have turned brown.

White chocolate almond protein drink

Servings: 1
Prep time: 2 minutes
Cook time: NA

Ingredients
- 8 ounces almond milk (unsweetened milk)
- ½ packet artificial sweetener
- 2 ounces heavy cream
- 1 scoop Vanilla Whey powder
- ½ tbsp. sugar free white chocolate syrup
- ½ cup crushed ice (you could add more or less as per your liking)

Method
1. Put all the ingredients in the blender and mix well. You have to ensure that the mixture is smooth.

Kale and Red Pepper Frittatas

Servings: 4
Prep time: 10 minutes
Cook time: 25 minutes

Ingredients

- 2 tbsp. coconut oil
- 1 cup red pepper (chopped)
- 2/3 cup onion (chopped)
- 6 slices bacon (chopped)
- 4 cups kale (chopped, rinsed and de – stemmed)
- 8 eggs
- ¼ cup coconut milk
- Salt and pepper to taste

Method

1. You will have to first preheat the oven to 350 degrees Fahrenheit.
2. Take a medium sized mixing bowl and add the eggs to it.
3. Whisk the eggs well to make sure that the yolk and the whites have been mixed well. Once that is done, you will need to add the coconut milk.
4. Whisk the mixture together and then add the salt and the pepper.
5. Set this mixture aside.
6. Place a skillet over medium heat. Once the skillet is warm, add the coconut oil. When the oil begins

to warm, add the onions. Cook the onions until they are translucent.

7. Next add the red peppers and sauté.
8. Now add the kale. Cook the vegetables until the kale begins to wilt.
9. Add the egg mixture to the skillet.
10. Add the bacon strips once the eggs have begun to cook.
11. Once the bottom of the frittata has started to set, remove the frittata off the gas and cook it in the oven for fifteen minutes.
12. Make sure that you cook the frittata all the way through. Cut the frittata into slices and serve

Banana Protein Shake

Servings: 2
Prep time: 5 minutes
Cook time: NA
Ingredients
- 4 ounces unsweetened almond milk
- 1 ounce heavy cream (low fat)
- ½ scoop Whey Isolate Powder
- 2 crushed bananas
- 1 cup crushed ice (Add as per your liking)
Method
1. Place all the ingredients in a blender. Now blend until a smooth and uniform mixture is obtained.

Healthy Smoothie

Servings: 6
Prep time: 10 minutes
Cook time: NA

Ingredients:

- 1 cup frozen strawberries
- 1 cup frozen raspberries
- 1 cup frozen blueberries
- 1 cup frozen blackberries
- 2 cups kale, stems, tough ribs removed, roughly chopped
- 2 cups spinach
- 1 cup orange segments
- 1 cup water
- 1/2 cup soft tofu

Method:

1. Place all the ingredients in a blender and blend until smooth and creamy.
2. Pour into tall glasses.
3. Serve

Green Smoothie

Servings: 2
Prep time: 10 minutes
Cook time: NA

Ingredients:
- 4 cups spinach
- 2 cups coconut milk, chilled, unsweetened
- 4 Brazil nuts
- 2/3 cup almonds
- 2 tablespoons psyllium husk
- 2 scoops whey protein powder
- 2 scoops greens powder
- 4 drops stevia or to taste (optional)

Method:
1. Place spinach, almonds, Brazil nuts and coconut milk to a blender and blend until smooth.
2. Add rest of the ingredients and blend until smooth and creamy.
3. Pour into tall glasses.
4. Serve immediately with crushed ice.

Breakfast Cereal Mix

Servings: 8-10
Prep time: 5 minutes
Cook time: NA

Ingredients:
- 10 tablespoons coconut flakes, unsweetened
- 14 tablespoons hemp seeds
- 10 tablespoons flaxseed, ground
- 4 tablespoons sesame, ground (grind for just a few seconds)
- 4 tablespoons dark cocoa, unsweetened
- 4 tablespoons psyllium husk
- 1 cup almonds, chopped

Method:
1. Mix together all the ingredients and place in an airtight container. Refrigerate until use.
2. To serve, add water or coffee or any nondairy milk, soak for a while and serve.

Pumpkin Pancakes

Servings: 6-8
Prep time: 15 minutes
Cook time: 3-5 minutes

Ingredients

- 2 pumpkins (shredded)
- 2 cups almond flour
- 3 eggs
- 2 tsp. dried basil
- 2 tsp. dried parsley
- Salt and Pepper to taste
- 3 tbsp. Butter

Method

1. Take a small mixing bowl and add the pumpkin, along with the basil and the almond flour.
2. Mix the ingredients well. Once the pumpkin is coated well with the flour, add the parsley, pepper and the salt to the bowl.
3. Ensure that the taste of the mixture is well balanced.
4. You can make close to 10 patties from the mixture that you have just made.
5. Take a large non – stick sauce pan and place it on a medium flame.
6. Add one teaspoon to the pan. Once the butter has started warming up, add the patties and cook them

one after the other.

7. Ensure that you remove the patty off the pan when it is brown on both sides.

Spicy Shrimp Omelet

Servings: 1-2
Prep time: 10 minutes
Cook time: 10 minutes

Ingredients:
- 3 eggs, whisked
- 2 grape tomatoes, halved
- 1 medium onion, chopped
- 5 shrimp, peeled, deveined
- 1 tablespoon fresh parsley, chopped
- 1/4 teaspoon cayenne pepper
- 1/8 teaspoon pepper powder
- 1/4 teaspoon salt or to taste
- 1 tablespoon coconut oil
- A dash of hot sauce

Method:
1. Place a nonstick pan over medium heat. Add oil. When oil melts, add onions and sauté until onions are translucent.
2. Add salt, pepper, cayenne pepper, shrimp and tomatoes. Sauté for a couple of minutes.
3. Pour whisked eggs over it. Sprinkle parsley. Cook until the eggs are set.
4. Drizzle hot sauce over it and serve.

Chapter 2: Ketogenic Appetizer Recipes

Buttered Brussels sprouts

Servings: 4-5
Prep time: 5 minutes
Cook time: 25 minutes

Ingredients:
- 1 pound Brussels sprouts
- 2 tablespoons lemon juice
- 2 ounces butter
- ½ teaspoon salt
- Freshly ground black pepper

Method:
1. Pre heat the oven to 400°F.
2. Wash the Brussels sprouts well and cut it into halves.
3. Pour the butter over the sprouts.
4. Sprinkle the lemon juice on the top of the sprouts.
5. Season it well with the salt and pepper and bake it in the oven for around twenty-five minutes. Serve warm.

Fried Cheese Sticks

Servings: 15
Prep time: 10 minutes
Cook time: 2-3 minutes

Ingredients:
- 15 cheese sticks, frozen (do not thaw)
- 2 eggs, beaten
- 4 tablespoons almond flour
- 2 tablespoons ground flax seeds
- 2 ounces parmesan, grated
- 1 teaspoon baking powder
- 2 tablespoons water
- Oil as required (coconut oil or olive oil)

Method:
1. Place a small, deep frying pan over medium heat. Add oil. It should cover at least 2 inches from the bottom of the pan. Heat until the temperature of oil is 375 degree F.
2. Meanwhile, mix together Parmesan, almond flour and baking powder in a bowl.
3. Add egg and water and beat well. Dip the frozen cheese sticks in this batter and immediately add to the hot oil. Cook until golden brown on all sides.
4. Remove with a slotted spoon and place on paper towels.
5. Serve with a low carb dip of your choice.

Fish Fingers

Servings: 8-10
Prep time: 15 minutes
Cook time: 4-5 minutes

Ingredients:
- 2 pounds fish like cod or snapper, rinsed, cut into fingers
- 4 eggs, beaten
- 1 cup shredded coconut
- Sea salt to taste
- 1 teaspoon garlic powder
- 1/2 teaspoon pepper powder to taste
- 1/2 cup coconut oil

Method:
1. Add coconut, salt, garlic powder and pepper powder to a bowl.
2. First dip the fingers in the egg and then roll in the coconut mixture and set aside on a plate.
3. Add 1/4-cup oil to a skillet and place the skillet over medium heat.
4. Add some of the fingers and cook until brown.
5. Repeat step 3 and 4 with the remaining fingers.
6. Serve with any dip of your choice.

Crab meat bites

Servings: 2-3
Prep time: 5 minutes
Cook time: 10 minutes

Ingredients:
- 1 can crab meat, drained
- 1/4 cup heavy cream
- 8 ounces softened cream cheese
- 1 tablespoon lemon juice
- 2 tablespoons finely chopped red bell pepper
- 2 tablespoons finely chopped onion
- 2 tablespoons finely chopped celery
- 1/2 teaspoon dry mustard
- 1/2 teaspoon salt

Method:
1. Mix all the ingredients well.
2. Transfer them into mini tart crusts.
3. Bake them in the oven for around ten minutes at 350 degrees F.

Cauliflower Breadsticks

Servings: 6-8
Prep time: 5 minutes
Cook time: 43-45 minutes

Ingredients:
- 1 large cauliflower head
- 1 ¼ cups of shredded Mozzarella cheese
- ¼ cup egg whites
- ¼ teaspoon freshly ground black pepper
- 1 teaspoon dried thyme
- Salt
- Marinara sauce

Method:
1. Pre heat the oven to 375°F.
2. Rinse the cauliflower well and cut it into florets. Toss it into the food processor and process it until it reaches the consistency of rice.
3. Bake the cauliflower in an oven for twenty minutes. Let it cool. Squeeze in the extra water from the cauliflower.
4. Increase the temperature of the oven to 450°F.
5. Mix the cauliflower, egg whites, and ½ cup of the shredded cheese, dried thyme, and black pepper, salt and combine well.
6. Flatten the cauliflower mixture on a baking sheet and bake it for around 18 minutes.
7. Add the remaining cheese and bake for another

five minutes. Broil it until the cheese turns golden brown.

8. Cut it into breadsticks and serve it with marinara sauce.

Taco Bites

Servings: 4-5
Prep time: 10 minutes
Cook time: 15 minutes

Ingredients:
- 1 pound ground beef
- 1/2 cup sour cream
- 2 tablespoons butter
- 1 yellow onion, chopped
- 3 cloves garlic, minced
- 2 teaspoons ground cumin
- 2 teaspoon chili powder
- 4 oz. can of green chilies
- 1 teaspoon ground coriander
- 2 to 3 cups grated cheddar cheese

Method:
1. In a skillet, fry the onions in the butter until they turn translucent.
2. Add the beef and cook until it is browned.
3. Add the spices and the chilies to the skillet and cook for another five minutes.
4. Reduce the heat and add the sour cream and cheese. Stir occasionally.
5. Spoon them into mini tart crusts.
6. Bake it in the oven for ten minutes at 350 degrees F.

Grain free taco shells

Servings: 12
Prep time: 2 minutes
Cook time: 11 minutes

Ingredients:
- 12 round slices of provolone cheese
- Chili powder
- Garlic powder

Method:
1. Pre heat the oven to 375°F.
2. Line a baking sheet with parchment paper. Place the cheese slices in an overlapping fashion.
3. Sprinkle the chili powder and garlic powder on top of the cheese slices.
4. Bake it in the oven for around eleven minutes until the cheese turns golden brown.
5. Let the cheese cool completely for it to harden. Your taco shells are now ready!

Healthy Granola Bars

Servings: 25-30
Prep time: 10 minutes
Cook time: 15 minutes

Ingredients:
- 3 cups macadamia nuts
- 3 cups almonds
- 3 cups sunflower seeds
- 3 cups unsweetened flaked coconut
- 3 eggs
- 3/4 cup coconut butter
- 3/4 cup organic peanut butter
- 1 1/2 cups dark chocolate chips
- 3 tablespoons vanilla extract
- 3 teaspoons pumpkin pie spice

Method:
1. Blend together all the ingredients in a blender until nutty or smooth. If you like them nutty, then make a coarse paste. If you like it smooth, then blend longer.
2. Transfer to a greased ovenproof dish. Press well.
3. Bake in a preheated oven at 350 degree F for 15 minutes or golden brown.
4. Cool slightly. Slice into pieces and serve.

Pizza Bites

Servings: 4-5
Prep time: 10 minutes
Cook time: 7-8 minutes

Ingredients:
- 3 ounce large pepperoni
- Pizza sauce as much as required
- Grated cheese as required (optional)
  For topping:
- Few olives, sliced
- 1 bell pepper, diced
- 3-4 mushrooms, chopped
- 1/2 cup green onions, chopped

Method:
1. Place the pepperoni slices on a lined baking sheet. Bake in a preheated oven at 400 degree F for about 7-8 minutes until the pepperoni is crisp.
2. Spread pizza sauce over each of the pepperoni. Sprinkle bell pepper, olives, mushrooms, green onions and cheese.
3. Bake for a few minutes until the cheese melts.

Teriyaki chicken wings

Servings: 6
Prep time: 8-10 minutes
Cook time: 15 minutes

Ingredients:
- 1 ½ pounds chicken wings
- 6 Tablespoon coconut aminos
- 2 to 3 tablespoons oil
- 2 Tablespoon equivalent sweetener
- 2 teaspoon ground ginger
- 1 teaspoon garlic powder
- ½ cup chicken broth
- Salt
- Black pepper

Method:
1. Toss the chicken wings with the oil, salt and pepper. Place it on a baking sheet that is lined with foil.
2. Set the oven broiler on high and cook the wings on the oven until both the sides are golden brown.
3. Mix the remaining ingredients in a saucepan over medium heat. Bring it to a boil and let it thicken.
4. Place the cooked wings in a bowl and pour the sauce over the wings. Serve hot.

Chapter 3: Ketogenic Soups and Salads

Egg salad

Servings: 4-6
Prep time: 10 minutes
Cook time: 15 minutes

Ingredients:
- 12 large eggs
- 1/2 cup mayonnaise
- 1/3 cup finely minced white onion
- 1/2 teaspoon ground mustard
- 2 tablespoons of melted butter
- 1 teaspoon black pepper
- 1 teaspoon salt

Method:
1. Pour in cold water into a large pot and place the eggs in it.
2. Bring it to a boil and cook it for ten minutes.
3. Drain out the hot water. Pour in some more cold water over the eggs.
4. Remove the eggs from the water and peel off the shells.
5. Cut the eggs into quarters. Mix in all the ingredients. Serve cold.

Lamb, cheese and cream Salad

Servings: 1
Prep time: 5 minutes
Cook time: NA

Ingredients:

For the Salad

- 1 cup diced lamb
- ½ cup diced celery
- 1 cup sliced tomato
- ½ cup sliced green onion

For the dressing

- 1 ounce mayonnaise
- ¼ tsp. thyme (dried)
- ¼ tsp. tarragon (dried)
- 1 ounce softened cream cheese
- Salt and pepper to taste

Method:

1. Whisk the cream cheese and mayonnaise to form a smooth mixture.
2. Add the spices to this mixture and whisk one more time.
3. Add the dry ingredients to a bowl and toss them well. Now, pour the dressing and toss the ingredients.

Peri Peri chicken Salad

Servings: 1
Prep time: 5 minutes
Cook time: 10 minutes

Ingredients:
- ½ Chicken breast
- 1 piece Low sodium bacon
- 2 cups Baby spinach
- Avocado (½ if small, 1/3 if a large fruit is taken)
- 1 table spoon Peri peri sauce

Method:
1. Slice the bacon and cook in a pan until it turns into a nice brown hue and becomes crispy.
2. Slice the chicken breast into pieces of even thickness.
3. Once the bacon is cooked, take it off the pan while retaining the fat in the pan.
4. Transfer the chicken slices into the pan and cook it on one side for approximately a minute.
5. Turn the pieces over and fry them well for 4 to 5 minutes.
6. While the chicken is being fried, slice the avocado into thin pieces.
7. Mix the avocado and spinach in a bowl and add the bacon and chicken pieces into it.
8. The final step is to add the peri peri sauce and mix the contents well.

Russian Slaw

Servings: 1-2
Prep time: 10 minutes
Cook time: NA

Ingredients:
- ¼ medium head green or white cabbage, shredded
- ¼ small head red cabbage, shredded
- ½ celeriac, peeled and grated
- ½ fennel bulb, shredded

For the Russian dressing:
- ⅓ cup mayonnaise
- 2 tablespoon freshly chopped chives
- 1 medium pickled cucumber, grated
- 2 tablespoon soured cream
- 1 teaspoon freshly grated horseradish
- 2 tablespoon fresh lemon juice
- 1 tablespoon Sriracha chili sauce
- 2 tablespoon freshly chopped parsley
- ¼ teaspoon salt
- Freshly ground black pepper

Method:
1. Mix the shredded cabbage, fennel with the grated celeriac.
2. Mix all the ingredients for the dressing well. Season it well with salt and pepper.

3. Add the dressing to the cabbage mixture. Mix well and serve.

Apple and Spinach Salad

Servings: 1-2
Prep time: minutes
Cook time: NA

Ingredients

- 2 cups spinach leaves (preferably baby spinach leaves. Ensure that they are washed well.)
- 1 cup red onion (sliced fine)
- 5 tbsp. blue cheese (crumbled)
- 1 apple (cut it into small cubes)

Method

1. Take a small bowl.
2. Add the apple cubes to the bowl.
3. Add the spinach to the bowl. Lay the onions on the spinach.
4. You could add your very own choice of dressing.

Beef stew and leeks

Servings: 4
Prep time: 20 minutes
Cook time: 25 minutes

Ingredients:
- 1 pound ground beef
- 2 cups chopped leeks
- 2 cups diced carrots
- 2 cups chopped onions
- 1 tsp. dried sage
- 1 cup chopped beans
- 1 cup chopped tomatoes
- 1 cup chopped mushrooms
- 1 cup chopped zucchini
- 1 cup cubed sweet potato
- 1 tsp. oregano
- 1 tbsp. olive oil
- 3 cups water
- Salt and pepper to taste

Method:
1. Add oil to a skillet placed on medium flame and sauté the onions until they have turned golden brown.
2. Add the ground beef to the pan and cook until the beef has browned.
3. Now, add the remaining ingredients to the pan and

continue to cook until you obtain a thick mixture.

4. Add the leeks to the pan and continue to cook until they have softened.

5. When the ingredients start to boil, cover the pan and simmer for a while. Serve hot.

Spicy Cauliflower soup

Servings: 2
Prep time: 10 minutes
Cook time: 15 minutes

Ingredients:
- 1/2 large cauliflower
- ½ medium turnip, peeled and finely diced
- 1 cup chicken stock
- ½ small white onion, finely chopped
- 1 ½ tablespoons butter
- ½ medium chorizo sausage, finely diced
- ½ medium spring onion
- ¼ teaspoon salt
- Cayenne pepper

Method:
1. Wash the cauliflower nicely and cut it into small pieces.
2. Use ¾ tablespoons butter to grease a large soup pot. Add in the finely chopped onions to the pot. Cook them until the onions turn golden brown.
3. Add in the cauliflower and cook it for another five minutes.
4. Pour in the chicken stock and cook it for ten minutes with the lid closed.
5. Grease a skillet with the remaining butter. Cook the chorizo and the turnip for around ten minutes.
6. Add half the chorizo and turnip mixture to the soup.

Blend the soup well with the help of a blender.
7. Season the soup with salt and cayenne pepper.
8. Garnish it with the spring onions and serve.

Spanish Sardines and Tomato Soup

Servings: 6
Prep time: 10 minutes
Cook time: 15 minutes

Ingredients:

- 9 ounces canned Spanish sardines in tomato sauce and olive oil
- 2 tablespoons olive oil
- 2 large tomatoes, sliced
- 4 cups fresh spinach
- 2 onions, sliced
- 2 cloves garlic, sliced
- 1 teaspoon black pepper powder
- 1 1/2 teaspoons salt or to taste
- 6 cups water

Method:

1. Place a large pot over medium heat. Add oil. When the oil is heated, add onions and garlic. Sauté until onions is softened.
2. Add tomatoes and sauté for a few minutes until tomatoes are soft.
3. Add sardines and sauté for a few minutes crushing the sardines simultaneously.
4. Add water and bring to a boil.
5. Lower heat and add spinach, salt and pepper. Let it simmer until spinach wilts.
6. Ladle soup into individual soup bowls and serve

hot.

Light Zucchini Soup

Servings: 2
Prep time: 8 minutes
Cook time: 13 minutes

Ingredients:
- 1 medium zucchini, chopped into cubes
- 2 cups vegetable stock
- 1 small onion, chopped
- 1 small chili pepper, chopped
- Salt to taste
- Pepper
- 1/4 cup fresh dill, chopped
- 1 tablespoon olive oil

Method:
1. Place a pot over medium heat. Add oil. When oil heats, add onions and pepper. Sauté until onions are translucent.
2. Add stock, salt, and pepper. Simmer for 8-10 minutes. Add zucchini and simmer further until tender. Remove from heat.
3. Add dill and serve either hot or cold. For cold, chill in the refrigerator.

Chilled Avocado Soup

Servings: 6
Prep time: 10 minutes
Cook time: NA

Ingredients:
- 3 cups Hass avocado puree
- 3 cups vegetable broth
- 3 cups heavy cream
- 1/2 cup cilantro, chopped
- 2 jalapeno peppers, deseeded, chopped
- 2 teaspoons ground cumin
- 1 teaspoon salt or to taste

Method:
1. Add all the ingredients to a food processor and blend until smooth.
2. Chill until use.
3. Serve in individual bowls.

Chapter 4: Ketogenic Vegetarian Recipes

Fettuccini Alfredo

Servings: 2
Prep time: 5 minutes
Cook time: 15 minutes

Ingredients:

For pasta:
- 4 eggs
- 1/8 teaspoon salt
- ¼ teaspoon pepper powder or to taste
- 2 ounces cream cheese
- 1/8 teaspoon garlic powder

For the sauce:
- 2 ounces mascarpone cheese
- 2 tablespoons butter
- 2 tablespoons parmesan cheese

Method:

1. To make pasta: Add all the ingredients of pasta into a blender and blend until smooth.
2. Pour into a large pan that is greased with butter.
3. Bake in a preheated oven at 350° F for about 8 minutes or the center is just set.
4. Remove from the oven and cool for 5 minutes. Pass a spatula at the underside of the cooked pasta sheet and loosen it.

5. Roll the whole sheet. Cut into 1/8 inch thick slices unroll the cut slices and set aside.
6. To make sauce: Add mascarpone cheese, Parmesan cheese and butter into a microwave safe bowl. Microwave on high for a minute. Remove from the microwave after 30 seconds and whisk until smooth. Place it back in the microwave and cook for the remaining 30 seconds.
7. Add the pasta and fold gently.
8. Serve immediately.

Cauliflower Rice

Servings: 4-6
Prep time: 10 minutes
Cook time: 10 minutes

Ingredients:
- 2 heads cauliflower, chopped into florets
- 1 onion, finely diced
- 4 tablespoons olive oil
- 4 cloves garlic, minced
- Salt to taste
- Pepper powder to taste

Method:
1. Add the cauliflower florets to the food processor and pulse until you get rice like texture. You can also grate the cauliflower.
2. Place a large nonstick skillet over medium high heat. Add oil. When oil is heated, add onions and sauté until translucent. Add garlic and sauté until fragrant.
3. Add cauliflower rice and sauté for about 5-6 minutes. Remove from heat.
4. Sprinkle salt and pepper just before serving.

Noodles with cucumber

Servings: 2
Prep time: 5 minutes
Cook time: 10 minutes

Ingredients:
- 2 cups peeled cucumber
- 3 cups water
- 4 tbsp. olive oil
- Salt, pepper, tomato sauce, soy sauce and chili to taste

Method:
1. Use the cucumber peels as noodles and place them in a pan with oil. Cook until they have become tender.
2. Add the water along with the needed spices to cook the cucumber noodles.
3. Cook the ingredients until the water has dried.
4. Add the sauce to the noodles and serve hot.

Grain free Mac and Cheese

Servings: 20-24
Prep time: 30 minutes
Cook time: 40-50 minutes

Ingredients:
- 1 cup crème fraiche
- 4 tablespoons yellow mustard
- 1 teaspoon pepper or to taste
- 1 teaspoon sea salt or to taste
- 1 cup onions, minced
- 12 pounds jicama, cut into 1 cm cubes
- 1 cup half and half
- 6 cups Sharp cheddar cheese, shredded

Method:
1. Add half and half, crème fraiche, salt, pepper and mustard into a bowl and mix well.
2. Add onion and jicama and mix well. Add cheese and mix until well combined.
3. Transfer into a greased baking dish.
4. Bake in a preheated oven at 350° F for about 40-50 minutes.
5. Remove from the oven and serve hot.

Bread Rolls

Servings: 4
Prep time: 5 minutes
Cook time: 45 minutes

Serves: 4
Ingredients:
- ¼ cup coconut oil, melted
- ½ teaspoon baking soda
- ½ teaspoon salt
- 12 tablespoons hot water
- 12 tablespoons coconut flour
- 2 tablespoons Italian seasoning
- 4 tablespoons gelatin
- Ghee or butter to serve

Method:
1. Add oil, coconut flour and baking soda into a bowl and mix well. Add Italian seasoning and salt.
2. Pour hot water into a bowl. Sprinkle gelatin on it. Mix well. Set aside for 2-3 minutes.
3. Add the gelatin mixture into the bowl of coconut flour and mix well to form dough.
4. Divide the dough into 4 equal portions. Shape into balls. Then roll the ball between the palms of your hands to a log shape.
5. Place on a greased baking sheet that is lined with parchment paper.
1. Bake in a preheated oven at 300°F for about 45

minutes.

6. Remove from oven and cool for a while. Brush with melted ghee or butter and serve.

Spinach Pie

Servings: 6
Prep time: 10 minutes
Cook time: 40 minutes

Ingredients:
- 1/4 cup butter
- 1/4 cup chopped onions
- 2 packages (16 ounces each) frozen chopped spinach, thawed, drained, squeezed of extra moisture
- 6 eggs
- 3 cups heavy cream
- 1 teaspoon salt
- 1 teaspoon black pepper powder
- 1 teaspoon ground nutmeg
- 1 cup Swiss cheese, shredded

Method:
1. Place a large saucepan over medium heat. Add most of the butter. When butter melts, add onions and sauté until the onions are translucent.
2. Add spinach. Cook until the mixture is almost dry. Transfer into a greased pie pan. Sprinkle cheese. Place blobs of remaining butter in 4-5 places.
3. Bake in a preheated oven for about 30 minutes.

Low Carb Pad Thai

Servings: 6
Prep time: 10 minutes
Cook time: NA

Ingredients:
- 2 packets kelp noodles
- 1 large onion, chopped
- 6 cloves garlic, minced
- 1 cup peanut butter
- 1/2 cup soy sauce or tamari
- 3 teaspoons red pepper flakes or to taste
- 1/4 cup lime juice
- 1 large carrot, peeled, shredded
- 2 scallions, chopped
- 2 tablespoons fresh cilantro, chopped
- 2 tablespoons sesame seeds, toasted

Method:
1. Place kelp noodles in a bowl and pour water over it. Set aside for it to soak.
2. Meanwhile, blend together onion, garlic, peanut butter, soy sauce, pepper flakes and lime juice until smooth.
3. When the noodles have soaked, drain the excess water.
4. Pour sauce over it. Sprinkle carrots, scallions, and cilantro and sesame seeds over it and serve.

Cheese Stuffed Portobello Mushrooms

Servings: 8
Prep time: 10 minutes
Cook time: 15-20 minutes

Ingredients:
- 8 Portobello mushrooms, remove stems and retain it
- 3 tablespoons fresh thyme, finely chopped
- 2 cups blue cheese, grated or crumbled
- 4 tablespoons extra virgin olive oil
- 4 cups lettuce finely chopped
- Pepper to taste
- Salt to taste

Method:
1. Finely chop the mushroom stems.
2. Mix together in a bowl, mushroom stems, cheese, 2 tablespoons thyme salt and pepper.
3. Stuff this mixture into the mushroom caps.
4. Place the mushroom caps on a baking sheet.
5. Bake in a preheated oven at 350°F for about 15-20 minutes.
6. Sprinkle remaining thyme on top and serve.
7. Place the lettuce leaves on a serving platter. Drizzle oil on it. Place the mushrooms on the lettuce.
8. Serve.

Oven Fried Green Beans

Servings: 4-5
Prep time: 15 minutes
Cook time: 15 minutes

Ingredients:
- 2 pounds fresh green beans, rinsed, trimmed
- 4 tablespoons olive oil + extra to grease the pan
- ½ cup parmesan cheese
- 2 teaspoons garlic powder
- Pepper to taste
- Salt to taste
- 2 eggs
- ½ cup almond flour
- 1 teaspoon paprika

Method:
1. Place aluminum foil in 2 baking dishes. Grease with a little oil.
2. Add eggs and oil in a bowl. Whisk well. Add green beans and mix until the beans are well coated in the mixture.
3. Transfer into the prepared dishes. Spread it all over the dish.
4. Bake in a preheated oven at 425°F for 15 minutes or until crisp.
5. Broil for a minute if desired.
6. Serve hot.

Italian Style Zucchini Rolls

Servings: 6
Prep time: 10 minutes
Cook time: 5 minutes

Ingredients:
- 6 small or baby zucchinis
- 2 cups soft goat's cheese
- 28 thin slices streaky bacon
- 1 cup sun dried tomatoes, drained, chopped
- 1 cup fresh basil
- ½ cup raspberry vinegar or any other fruit vinegar

Method:
1. Make thin strips of the zucchinis using a peeler.
2. Add vinegar into a bowl. Add zucchini strips into the bowl. The strips should dip into the vinegar. Set aside for about 10 minutes.
3. Meanwhile line a baking sheet with parchment paper. Place bacon strips on the baking sheet.
4. Bake in a preheated oven at 400° F for 5 minutes or until slightly crisp.
5. Remove from the oven.
6. Lay the zucchini strips on your work area. Place a strip of bacon on each zucchini strip. Sprinkle cheese on it. Place a piece of tomato and sprinkle basil on it. Roll each set. Insert a toothpick in each.
7. Serve.

Chapter 5: Ketogenic Main Course Recipes

Ground beef stir fry

Servings: 1
Prep time: 10 minutes
Cook time: 10 minutes

Ingredients:
- ½ pound Ground beef
- 5 Brown mushrooms, medium size
- ½ cup Broccoli
- ½ Spanish onion, medium size
- 1/2 tablespoon Coconut oil
- 1 tablespoon Chinese Five Spices
- 1 tablespoon Cayenne pepper
- ½ Red pepper, medium size
- 2 Kale leaves

Method:
1. Slice and chop the broccoli, mushrooms, red pepper and kale.
2. Take a large to medium sized skillet and fry the onions in coconut oil for about one minute. The flame should be medium to high.
3. Once the onions turn golden brown, add the rest of the vegetables and stir-fry for another 2 minutes.
4. Into the pan, add the ground beef and cook for another 2 minutes.

5. Now turn down the heat to medium, cover the skillet and let it cook until the beef turns a brown hue. This shouldn't take you more than 10 minutes.

Zucchini Casserole

Servings: 6
Prep time: 15 minutes
Cook time: 20 minutes

Ingredients:
- 12 cups zucchini, diced
- 1 red bell pepper chopped
- 1 yellow bell pepper, chopped
- 1 cup quinoa, cook according to the package instructions
- 1 1/2 cups cheddar cheese, shredded
- 3/4 cup olive oil
- 1 1/2 teaspoons dried basil
- 3 eggs, beaten
- Salt to taste
- Pepper powder to taste

Method:
1. Mix together all the ingredients in a bowl. Transfer to a greased baking dish.
2. Spread the mixture all over.
3. Bake in a preheated oven at 350 degree F until top is golden brown.

Lemon garlic fish

Servings: 4
Prep time: 5 minutes
Cook time: 2 minutes

Ingredients:
- 4 tilapia fillets
- 2 medium lemon
- 2 garlic cloves
- 2 tablespoons olive oil
- ¼ teaspoon salt
- ½ bunch fresh parsley
- Freshly ground black pepper

Method:
1. Clean the parsley well and put the leaves into a food processor.
2. Cut the lemons into two halves and add the juice and zest from one lemon to the food processor.
3. Add the garlic, olive oil, salt and pepper. Turn on the processor and mince the garlic and the parsley well.
4. Keep the fish fillers on a bowl. Apply the parsley mixture on both the sides of the fillets.
5. Place the fillets on a preheated grill and cook it for two minutes until the fish is browned.
6. Serve it hot with the remaining lemon slices.

Keto Italian Meatballs

Servings: 4-5
Prep time: 30 minutes
Cook time: 30-45 minutes

Ingredients
- 8 ounces minced white onion
- 4 teaspoons Italian seasoning
- 3 teaspoons sea salt
- 1 ½ teaspoons freshly ground black pepper
- 2 cup shredded parmesan / Romano / asiago mix
- 2 pounds ground beef (ensure it is 92% lean)
- 2 tablespoons olive oil
- 2 cups cold whole milk ricotta cheese
- 2 large eggs
- 3 teaspoons granulated garlic

Procedure
1. Preheat the oven to 350 degrees Celsius.
2. Heat a saucepan on a medium flame and add the olive oil followed by the onions. Sauté the onions in the oil until they turn translucent.
3. Remove the saucepan from the flame, and let it cool down for ten minutes.
4. Take the shredded Parmesan / Romano / asiago and mince it in your food processor.
5. In a large mixing bowl, add the ricotta cheese and the egg. Whisk this mixture until there are no

lumps and the mixture is smooth.

6. Add the spices, salt and pepper to this mix. Stir well to ensure that the spices have spread evenly through the mixture.

7. Add the onions to the mixture followed by the minced Parmesan. Mix the ingredients well, together.

8. Once the mixture has been made, add the beef to the mixture. Ensure that all the ingredients have complemented each other and the taste is the same throughout the mixture.

9. Divide the mixture into 2-ounce portions. You will end up with close to 40 equal sized pieces.

10. Roll each of these pieces into a ball.

11. Take a cookie sheet and coat it with butter or oil. Place the meatballs on the tray and bake at 350 degrees. They are cooked in about twenty minutes. They should be brown.

Chicken chowder

Servings: 5-6
Prep time: 20 minutes
Cook time: 20 minutes

Ingredients:
- 2 cups pound beef
- 3 cups pound chicken
- 2 cups chopped carrots
- 3 cups cauliflower florets
- 1 cup chopped celery
- 1 tsp. ground coriander
- 5 cups vegetable stock
- 2 cups coconut milk
- 1 cup diced onions
- 1 tsp. turmeric powder
- 2 tsp. sliced garlic
- 2 tbsp. chopped dill
- 2 tsp. ground cinnamon
- 1 tbsp. olive oil
- Salt and pepper to taste

Method:
1. Add oil to a saucepan placed on medium flame. You will need to cook the onions until they have turned golden brown.
2. Cook the ground meat until it has browned on all sides.

3. Add the other vegetables to the pan and continue to cook until the vegetables have become soft.
4. You will need to add the stock to the pan and continue to cook until the ingredients have boiled.
5. Lower the flame and continue to simmer. When the vegetables have become tender, turn off the heat. Garnish with dill and serve hot.

Ground Beef and Spinach Skillet

Servings: 2-3
Prep time: 15 minutes
Cook time: 20 minutes

Ingredients:
- 4 tablespoons coconut oil or ghee
- 2 king oyster mushrooms, chopped
- 4 tablespoons raw almonds, chopped
- 3/4 pound lean ground beef
- 1/2 teaspoon chili pepper flakes
- A large pinch Himalayan salt
- A large pinch ground white pepper
- 1/2 cups pitted Kalamata olives
- 2 tablespoons capers
- 2 tablespoons natural roasted almond butter
- 3/4 pound baby spinach leaves, roughly chopped

Method:
1. Place a heavy bottomed skillet over medium high heat. Add coconut oil. When oil melts, add mushrooms and sauté until brown.
2. Add almonds and sauté for a minute. Add beef, salt, white pepper powder, chili pepper flakes and cook until the meat is brown and cooked well.
3. Add olives, capers and almond butter. Mix well. Add spinach and sauté for a couple of minutes until the spinach wilts well.
4. Serve immediately.

Spicy Shrimp with Chilies and Garlic

Servings: 3
Prep time: 15 minutes
Cook time: 7 minutes

Ingredients:

- 1 ½ pounds Shrimp, medium, deveined and peeled
- 1 tablespoon Parsley, fresh and chopped
- 5 Garlic cloves, crushed
- Freshly ground Black pepper, ground
- Kosher salt
- 1 Lemon juice
- 3 to 4 Dried Chilies, dried and cut
- 1 tablespoon Olive oil, extra virgin

Method:

1. The shrimp has to be seasoned with the black pepper and kosher salt as per r taste.
2. Take a large skillet and heat it over a medium flame. Add half a teaspoon of the oil.
3. Once the oil is hot, add half of the chilies and cook it for about 2 minutes.
4. It's time for the shrimp. Turn the heat up to medium high and add half the shrimp. The other half has to be saved for the next step. The shrimp has to be cooked for 2 to 3 minutes. You have to turn them over half way through. The shrimps are done when they are opaque. Transfer the contents

to a plate.

5. Now repeat the above step. That is, add the balance of the oil, chilies and shrimp and cook for about 1 ½ to 2 minutes.

6. Turn the shrimp over and when it looks almost done, add the garlic and cook for another minute.

7. Now add the first batch back into the skillet and mix the contents well so that garlic is spread out evenly.

8. Turn off the heat and pour the lemon juice over the shrimp. Add the parsley and mix it well. And there you have your spicy shrimp with chilies and garlic.

Glazed Pork Tenderloin

Servings: 2
Prep time: 5 minutes
Cook time: 60 minutes

Ingredients
- 1 pound Pork Tenderloin
- 2 tbsp. Maple Syrup
- 2 tbsp. olive oil
- 2 tbsp. Balsamic vinegar
- 2 tbsp. dried thyme
- 1 tsp. paprika
- Salt and Pepper to taste

Method
1. You will first need to make a marinade for the pork. Use all the ingredients that have been mentioned aside from the pork to make the marinade.
2. Mix the ingredients well. You can use a whisk to ensure that there are no lumps.
3. Now place the pork in the marinade and make sure that all the sides of the marinade are coated.
4. Leave the pork in a freezer bag. Allow it to marinade for a minimum of ten hours.
5. When the time is up, place the pork tenderloin in the oven.
6. You can bake it at 180 degree Celsius. Make sure that the bake time is 40 minutes.

7. Add the remaining marinade to a saucepan. Place it on a low flame.
8. Let the marinade thicken. Once it has thickened, switch off the heat.
9. Remove the pork from the oven and checked if it is cooked or not. If it is cooked, add it to the thickened sauce.
10. Place it in the oven and cook for another five minutes.
11. Set it aside for ten minutes
12. Serve with roasted vegetables.

Seafood stew

Servings: 8
Prep time: 20 minutes
Cook time: 20 minutes

Ingredients:
- 1 cup chopped shrimp
- 1 cup chopped salmon
- 1 cup chopped carp
- 2 cups chopped kingfish
- 2 cups chopped leeks
- 2 cups diced carrots
- 2 cups chopped onions
- 1 tsp. dried sage
- 1 cup chopped beans
- 1 cup chopped tomatoes
- 1 cup chopped mushrooms
- 1 cup chopped zucchini
- 1 cup cubed sweet potato
- 1 tsp. oregano
- 1 tbsp. olive oil
- 3 cups water
- Salt and pepper to taste

Method:
1. Add oil to a skillet placed on medium flame and sauté the onions until they have turned golden brown.

2. Add the chopped fish to the pan and remove immediately after cooked.
3. Now, add the remaining ingredients to the pan and continue to cook until you obtain a thick mixture.
4. When the ingredients start to boil, cover the pan and simmer for a while. Add the fish and cook for five minutes.
5. Serve hot.

Sri Lankan Fish Curry

Servings: 6
Prep time: 5 minutes
Cook time: 30 minutes

Ingredients:

- 6 pieces (about 2 pounds) Silver Hake or any other white fish
- 6 tablespoons coconut oil
- 1/2 teaspoon whole mustard seeds
- 3 long green chilies, deseeded, cut in small pieces
- 1 onion, finely chopped
- 1/2 tablespoon fresh ginger, grated
- 1/2 teaspoon ground cumin
- 1/2 tablespoon curry powder
- 1 teaspoon turmeric powder
- 5 cloves of garlic, chopped
- 2 1/2 cups full fat coconut cream
- 1 teaspoon sea salt
- Chopped cilantro to garnish
- 3/4 cup water

Method:

1. Place a large saucepan over medium heat. Add half the coconut oil. When the oil is melted, add mustard seeds. In a while, it will start spluttering. When the sound of spluttering reduces, add onions and sauté for a few minutes.
2. Add ginger and garlic. Sauté for 4-5 minutes.

3. Add green chilies, curry powder, cumin powder and turmeric. Sauté for a couple of minutes more.
4. Add coconut milk and salt. Mix well and bring to a boil.
5. Reduce heat and simmer for about 15 minutes.
6. Meanwhile, add rest of the oil to a nonstick pan. Place the pan over medium heat.
7. Add fish to it and fry for 2 -3 minutes. When the underside is cooked, flip sides and cook the other side too.
8. Add fish to the simmering curry. Simmer for another 5-7 minutes.
9. Garnish with cilantro and serve.

Lamb Souvlaki (Greek Lamb Skewers)

Servings: 5-6
Prep time: 5 minutes
Cook time: 30 minutes

Ingredients:
- 2 1/2 pounds lamb, chopped into medium size pieces
- 1/2 cup fresh mint, chopped or 2 teaspoons dried mint
- 3 tablespoons fresh rosemary, chopped or 2 teaspoons dried rosemary
- Juice of 2 lemons
- 3/4 cup extra virgin olive oil
- 1 teaspoon salt or to taste
- Melitzanosalata (eggplant dip) to serve

Method:
1. Add olive oil and lemon juice to a large bowl. Add salt, mint, and rosemary to it and mix well.
2. Add the lamb pieces and mix well. Marinate in the refrigerator overnight. Toss it a couple of times in between or more often.
3. Thread the meat pieces on to skewers. Place the skewers on the rack in a preheated oven.
4. Roast at 450 degree F until done. Turn the skewers around a couple of times in between.
5. Remove from the oven. Let it cool for a couple of

minutes. Remove from the skewers.
6. Serve with Melitzanosalata.

Chicken in Butter Gravy

Servings: 4-6
Prep time: 10 minutes
Cook time: 45 minutes

Ingredients:
- 1 1/2 pounds chicken thighs with bones
- 1/2 cup water
- 1/2 cup pureed tomatoes
- 1/4 cup heavy cream
- 3 tablespoons butter
- 1/2 tablespoon olive oil
- 1 teaspoon coconut oil
- 3/4 teaspoon ginger paste
- 3/4 teaspoon garlic paste
- 1/2 teaspoon coriander, ground
- Salt to taste
- 1/2 teaspoon garam masala powder (Indian spice blend)
- 1/4 teaspoon Kashmiri chili powder
- 1/2 teaspoon paprika
- 1/2 teaspoon red chili powder
- Cilantro for garnishing, chopped
- Cauliflower rice to serve

Method:
1. Rub the chicken thighs with olive oil, salt, and pepper. Keep aside for 15-20 minutes.

2. Roast in a preheated oven at 375 degree F for about 25 minutes or until almost cooked (it should not be fully cooked).
3. When almost cooked, remove from the oven, cool. Remove the bones from the pieces and keep aside.
4. Place butter and coconut oil in a medium sized pan over medium heat.
5. When butter melts, add ginger and garlic paste. Sauté for a couple of minutes. Add tomatoes, coriander powder, chili powder, garam masala, paprika, and Kashmir chili powder. Simmer for a while until the butter is visible on the top.
6. Add the chicken pieces, cream, and water and simmer for another 5 minutes more.
7. Serve hot garnished with cilantro leaves. Serve with cauliflower rice.

Ground Pork Tacos

Servings: 4-6
Prep time: 15 minutes
Cook time: 20 minutes

Ingredients:
- 2 pounds ground pork
- 1 1/2 teaspoons garlic powder
- 1 1/2 teaspoons onion powder
- 1 teaspoon sea salt
- 1 teaspoon ground cumin
- 1/2 teaspoon ground pepper or to taste
- 1/4 cup salsa
- 15 large lettuce leaves or more if required
- 3/4 cup green bell pepper, chopped
- 3/4 cup red bell pepper, chopped
- 2 medium onions, chopped

Method:
1. Add pork, garlic powder, onion powder, salt, cumin, and pepper to a skillet. Mix well using your hands.
2. Place the skillet over medium heat. Stir constantly and cook until the pork is browned well.
3. Remove the pork with a slotted spoon and place in a bowl. Discard the remaining fat.
4. Add salsa and mix well. Taste and adjust the seasonings if necessary.

5. Lay the lettuce leaves on your working area. Place some pork filling at the center.
6. Sprinkle peppers, and onions. Wrap it up and serve.

Baked Salmon

Servings: 2
Prep time: 5 minutes
Cook time: 50 minutes

Ingredients

- 4 cloves garlic
- 12 tbsp. olive oil (light)
- 2 tsp. basil (dried)
- 2 tsp. salt
- 2 tsp. black pepper (ground)
- 2 tbsp. lemon juice
- 2 tbsp. fresh parsley (chopped)
- 12 ounces salmon fillets

Method

1. Preheat the oven 375 degree Fahrenheit.
2. Take a medium sized bowl and add the garlic, olive oil, salt, basil and the pepper and mix well. Make sure that the taste has spread evenly throughout the mixture. Add the lemon juice and the parsley to the mixture.
3. Take a baking dish and add the salmon fillets. Cover the fillets with the marinade and leave them for an hour. Turn the fillets over.
4. Place the salmon in an aluminum foil and seal the salmon in it.
5. Place the salmon in a baking dish and leave it in

the oven for fifty minutes to cook.
6. Serve hot.

Beef and mixed vegetable Stir Fry

Servings: 3
Prep time: 10 minutes
Cook time: 20 minutes

Ingredients

- 1 lb. beef
- 2 tbsp. coconut oil
- 1 cup onion minced
- 2 cups broccoli chopped
- 1 tbsp. sesame seeds
- 3 tbsp. green onion chopped
- 1 cup chestnuts sliced

Method

1. First, clean the beef and cut it into small pieces of equal size.
2. Place a pan over medium flame. Add the coconut oil to the pan and wait for it to heat.
3. Once the coconut oil is hot, you will need to put the beef in the pan.
4. Cook the beef and make sure that it is brown on all sides.
5. Remove the beef from the pan and set it aside.
6. Add the onion and the broccoli to the pan and sauté for a few minutes. You need to make sure that the onion is translucent and that the broccoli begins to wilt.

7. Add the beef to the pan and fry for a few minutes. Once the flavors bend together. You could add more vegetables to the dish if you like

Stir Fried Bacon & Vegetables

Servings: 4
Prep time: 15 minutes
Cook time: 15 minutes

Ingredients:

- 10 strips smoked bacon, chopped into fine pieces
- 2 cups kale, discard hard stems and ribs
- 1 medium head broccoli, chopped into florets
- 1 red bell pepper, sliced
- 1 cup green beans, chopped into 1 inch pieces
- 2 small courgettes, chopped
- 2 cloves garlic, chopped
- 2 teaspoons butter
- 2 teaspoons coconut oil
- Salt to taste
- Pepper powder to taste
- 1 cup thick single cream
- Cauliflower rice to serve

Method:

1. Place a skillet over medium heat. Add coconut oil and butter. When it melts, add garlic and sauté until fragrant.
2. Add all the vegetables, salt and pepper and sauté until the vegetables are crisp and tender as well.
3. Add bacon and stir for a couple of minutes. Remove from heat. Add cream and mix.
4. Serve over cauliflower rice.

Chicken and cheese enchilada

Servings: 6
Prep time: 10 minutes
Cook time: 15 minutes

Ingredients:
- 3 cups mixed vegetables
- 2 lb. ground chicken
- 1 cup melted cheese
- ½ cup chopped shallots
- 2 tortillas
- 1 tbsp. butter

Method:
1. Melt butter on a skillet placed on medium flame.
2. Add the shallots and chicken to the skillet. Sauté until the shallots have turned golden brown and are translucent.
3. Toss the ingredients.
4. Transfer this mixture onto the tortilla and roll it. Add the molten cheese.
5. Serve with a mayonnaise dip.

Pork and Beef bake

Servings: 4
Prep time: 10 minutes
Cook time: 50 minutes

Ingredients:
- 1 tbsp. fresh parsley (chopped)
- 2 cloves garlic
- 6 tbsp. olive oil (light)
- 3 tsp. basil (dried)
- 1 pound ground pork
- 1 pound ground beef
- 1 tsp. black pepper (ground)
- 1 tsp. salt
- 1 tbsp. lemon juice

Method:
1. Preheat the oven to 300 degrees Fahrenheit.
2. Add the garlic, oil, pepper, basil and the salt in a bowl and mix well. Now, add the lemon juice and the parsley to the bowl.
3. Pour the marinade over the pork and the beef. Leave the fillets for an hour in the refrigerator.
4. Prepare a baking dish with aluminum foil and add the meat to it. Cover the meat well with the foil.
5. Cook the meat for fifty minutes in the oven.

Spicy Chicken Nuggets

Servings: 2
Prep time: 20 minutes
Cook time: 20 minutes

Ingredients:
- 1 ounce pork rinds
- 16 ounces chicken tenders, chop into bite sized pieces
- 2 tablespoons almond flour
- 1 egg, beaten
- 1/4 teaspoon chili powder
- Cayenne pepper to taste
- 1/4 teaspoon garlic powder
- 1/2 teaspoon onion powder
- 1/4 teaspoon Creole seasoning
- Salt to taste
- Pepper powder to taste

Method:
1. Blend together pork rind, onion and garlic powder, Creole seasoning, almond flour, salt, pepper, chili powder and cayenne pepper in a blender. Transfer into a bowl.
2. First dip a chicken nugget in egg and then in the almond flour mixture. Place on a greased baking sheet. Repeat with the remaining nuggets.
3. Bake in a preheated oven at 400 degree F for 20 minutes or until brown and crisp.

Chapter 6: Ketogenic Dessert Recipes

Raspberry Chia Pudding

Servings: 1
Prep time: 2 minutes
Cook time: NA

Ingredients:
- 1/2 cup vanilla flavored almond milk or soy milk, unsweetened
- 1/2 scoop vanilla protein powder
- 2 tablespoons raspberries, fresh or frozen
- 1 1/2 tablespoons chia seeds

Method:
1. Whisk together almond milk and protein powder.
2. Add chia seeds and mix well. Keep aside for 5-7 minutes. Stir again.
3. Repeat step 2.
4. Mix raspberries in it.
5. Keep aside for an hour in the refrigerator.

Coconut Cream Macaroons

Servings: 10-12
Prep time: 20 minutes
Cook time: 25 minutes

Ingredients:
- 4 large egg whites
- 16 ounces unsweetened dried coconut, finely shredded
- 1 teaspoon vanilla
- 8 ounces softened cream cheese
- 2 ounces heavy cream
- 1 cup erythritol
- 1/8 teaspoon salt
- ¼ teaspoon cream of tartar
- 2 ounces semi sweet mini chocolate chips
- 2 ounces sugar free white chocolate syrup

Method:
1. Pre heat the oven to 325 degree F.
2. Line two cookie sheets with parchment paper.
3. Add the egg whites, cream of tartar, vanilla and salt to a large bowl and mix it with the help of an electric mixer until they turn into soft peaks.
4. Pour in the erythritol into the bowl, one tablespoon at a time and beat well. Fold in the shredded coconut.
5. Beat the heavy cream and the cream cheese well. Pour in the syrup and mix well. Add the coconut

mixture and combine well. Add the chocolate chips to it.

6. Scoop out the mixture and line it neatly on the cookie sheets. Bake it in the oven for around 25 minutes. Let it cool completely and serve.

Lemon Cheesecake

Servings: 12-15
Prep time: 5 minutes
Cook time: NA

Ingredients

- 16 ounces cream cheese (softened at room temperature)
- 4 ounces heavy cream
- 2 tsp. Stevia Glycerite
- 2 tsp. Splenda (or any other artificial sweetener which is low in carbohydrates)
- 2 tbsp. lemon juice
- 2 tsp. vanilla essence or flavoring

Method

1. Add all the ingredients in a large mixing bowl.
2. Whisk them well until it has a consistency that is pudding like.
3. Spoon the batter into small cups and leave it in the refrigerator to set.

Berry Ice Cream

Servings: 8-10
Prep time: 5 minutes
Cook time: NA

Ingredients:
- 3 cups heavy whipping cream
- 1 1/2 cups blueberries or strawberries, or any other berries of your choice, unsweetened + extra for garnishing
- Few drops of stevia sweetener or any other sweetener of your choice (optional)

Method:
1. Add all the ingredients to a blender. Blend until smooth.
2. Freeze the ice cream for 5-6 hours or until set.
3. Remove from the freezer around 30 minutes before serving.
4. Garnish with the berries that you are using.

Chocolate and Peanut Butter Bites

Servings: 16-20
Prep time: 10 minutes
Cook time: NA

Ingredients:
- 4 large Hass avocadoes, peeled, pitted, chopped
- 1/2 cup peanut butter, unsweetened
- 1/2 cup cocoa powder
- 20 drops liquid stevia or to taste (optional)

Method:
1. Blend together all the ingredients except peanut butter until smooth and creamy.
2. Pour into a freezer safe container. Add peanut butter. With a knife, swirls the peanut butter.
3. Freeze until done.
4. Remove from the freezer 15 minutes before serving.
5. Scoop and serve.

White Chocolate Raspberry Cheesecake

Servings: 15-20
Prep time: 5 minutes
Cook time: NA

Ingredients:
- 16 ounces softened cream cheese
- 2 teaspoons Stevia Glycerite
- 4 ounces heavy cream
- 2 teaspoons raspberry preserves
- 2 tablespoons sugar free white chocolate syrup.

Method:
1. Take all the ingredients in a large bowl. Mix well until it reaches the consistency of a pudding.
2. Transfer it to small serving cups. Refrigerate the cups until it is set.

Gluten free Blueberry Crisp

Servings: 8
Prep time: 10 minutes
Cook time: 30 minutes

Ingredients
- 2 cups fresh blueberries
- 1 tsp. lemon juice
- 1½ cup almond flour
- 1 cup almonds (slivered)
- ½ cup coconut oil (melted)
- 3 tbsp. maple syrup
- 1½ tsp. cinnamon
- ¼ tsp. salt
- Pinch of nutmeg

Method
1. You will first need to preheat your oven to 375 degrees Fahrenheit.
2. Take a small mixing bowl and add the blueberries and the lemon juice. Toss the blueberries well to ensure that they are covered well with the lemon juice.
3. Take six ramekin dishes and divide the blueberries in them.
4. In the same mixing bowl, add the other ingredients and make sure that they are all mixed well. You have to ensure that the almond crumble is mixed

well.

5. Scoop the almond crumble well and place it over the blueberries.
6. Bake this in the oven until the almond crumble is golden brown. This takes half an hour.
7. Cool the dish at room temperature.
8. Serve it cold.

Vanilla Pudding

Servings: 6
Prep time: 5 minutes
Cook time: NA

Ingredients:
- 16 ounces softened cream cheese
- 8 to 12 drops of liquid Stevia
- 8 ounces heavy whipping cream
- 2 tablespoons of sugar free vanilla syrup

Method:
1. Mix all the ingredients well.
2. Transfer the mixture to six serving bowls.
3. Refrigerate the bowls until the pudding is set. Serve cold.

Chocolate Cherry Cheesecake

Servings: 12-15
Prep time: 5 minutes
Cook time: NA

Ingredients
- 16 ounces cream cheese (softened at room temperature)
- 4 ounces heavy cream
- 2 tsp. Stevia Glycerite
- 2 tsp. Splenda (or any other artificial sweetener which is low in carbohydrates)
- 2 tbsp. Dutch processed cocoa powder
- 2 tbsp. Sugar free cherry syrup

Method
1. Add all the ingredients in a large mixing bowl.
2. Whisk them well until it has a consistency that is pudding like.
3. Spoon the batter into small cups and leave it in the refrigerator to set.

Rich chocolate muffin

Servings: 15-20
Prep time: 10 minutes
Cook time: 30 minutes

Ingredients
- 3 cups almond flour
- 2 cups heavy cream
- 3 large eggs
- 1 cup melted butter
- 1 cup xylitol
- 2 tsp. vanilla extract
- 2 tsp. baking soda
- ½ tsp. salt
- 1 cup chocolate chips (ensure that the brand you choose has low carbohydrates)

Method
1. Preheat the oven to 300° Fahrenheit.
2. Keep the muffin covers in each hole of the muffin pan.
3. Take a small bowl and add the cream and the almond flour. Whisk the two ingredients together.
4. Add the eggs one at a time and keep stirring until the mixture has become smooth.
5. Add the butter, baking soda, sweetener, flavoring and the salt to the bowl. Mix all the ingredients together.
6. Add the chocolate to the bowl and stir the

ingredients together until they are distributed evenly.

7. Take the mixture and place it in each of the muffin holes. Bake the cupcakes for thirty minutes. Leave them in the oven until they are golden brown.

8. Let them cool down. Serve them with butter.

Conclusion

I would like to thank you once again for purchasing this book.

The recipes that have been mentioned in this book are easy to follow. The next time you have your friends or family over for a meal, you can surprise them with any of the recipes mentioned in this book. All that you will need to do is gather all the necessary ingredients well in advance.

The ketogenic diet is a wonderful diet. It isn't difficult to follow. There are a few things that you will need to keep in mind if you are serious about following this diet. Make sure that you always have keto friendly ingredients stored in your pantry. You should always shop in advance for groceries and plan your meals. You will need to be patient and don't expect any quick results. Resist your urge to giving into any carb cravings. If you are craving for something sweet, try finding an alternative to replacing that craving with.

Thank you and all the best for your diet!

Intermittent Fasting

The Ultimate Guide To Staying Lean And Healthy While Eating The Foods You Love!

Free Bonus

I want to thank you for purchasing this book, hence I would like to give you a free gift in return. <u>Click here</u> or follow the link below to claim your free gift now.
Cheers!

http://eepurl.com/cRXcDf

Introduction

There's a reason why intermittent fasting's one of the most popular eating plans in the world today: It works! More specifically, it helps people not just lose the right kind of weight (which you'll learn about in the book) but also become and stay healthy. While it's not a magic pill to make all your flab and sicknesses go away, it can help you achieve your ideal weight and significantly reduce your risks of certain major health conditions.

In this book, I'll show you what intermittent fasting really is, why you should incorporate it into your lifestyle, how it can help you get and stay lean and healthy, the different ways of fasting intermittently (protocols) and how to live the intermittent fasting lifestyle with a list of things you should and shouldn't do. By the time you finish reading this book, you'll be in a great position to start incorporating intermittent fasting into your lifestyle and be on your way to becoming lean and healthier.

If you're ready, turn the page and let's begin!

Chapter 1: Intermittent Fasting Basics

In order to fully understand what intermittent fasting is and why you can benefit much from it as part of your lifestyle, it's important to dissect the term into its component words – fasting and intermittent. Let's talk about fasting first.

A lot of people have many different impressions about the word "fasting." For some people, it's a diet. For some, it's a way of twisting the arm of God to get what they want from Him – as if they can twist God's arm. For some, it's a way of cleansing the body. So what is fasting, really?

Basically, fasting is the act of intentionally staying away from food for a specific period of time. A person can fast – or stay away from food – completely or partially. The reason for many people's perception about fasting as a means of obtaining the favor of God is because of its strong associations with major religions such as Christianity, Judaism and Islam. With these and other religions, fasting is one of the best ways to "please" God (whether the intention is to merely please Him or obtain His blessings), to pay for the sins they've committed, or to make their spirits stronger and more sensitive to God's voice.

The latter perception of spiritual strengthening and sharpening is surprisingly backed up by psychological principles, albeit from a different angle. How's that so?

For people who are very religious or devout, the ability to resist the world's temptations such as sex, vices and materialism, among others, is dependent on the strength of one's spirit. There's a very good spiritual analogy that illustrates the battle between the spirit and the flesh or worldly desires – the good and evil inner wolves.

The Native American Indians believe that within a person's spirit live 2 wolves, both of whom are at odds with each other. The stronger wolf is the one that makes the person think, feel and live their lives in a particular way, i.e., good or bad. And who determines who between the two wolves is stronger? The person himself.

If a person starves his fleshly wolf, the evil one, he weakens it and inadvertently feeds the good wolf to make it strong, and vice versa. Fasting is one of the major ways that most religions feed the good wolf and consequently, starve the evil one. That's why religious people believe that fasting helps strengthen the spirit, i.e., the good wolf, to fight against temptation.

In the field of psychology, the term used to refer to the practice of starving the evil wolf is delayed gratification. If you recall what happened in the now famous marshmallow test conducted on children, those who were able to resist the lure of eating the marshmallows immediately grew up to be generally well-adjusted and disciplined adults. Since fasting involves a lot of delayed gratification, it allows a person to develop a much stronger character or will power.

Why Go Hungry?

Believe it or not, the benefits of fasting aren't just limited to the spirit or the psyche. It also extends to the physical body. Now, how can going hungry for a relatively long period of time be of any physical benefit when most of what popular science says about going hungry for long periods of time isn't all that good? Further, isn't it that food is one of the essential requirements for longevity?

While it's true that food is a requirement for staying alive and hunger is generally not good for the body and mind, intentionally going hungry for a limited period of time, done the right way, can actually make a person much, much healthier both physically and mentally. The key to this is fasting intermittently, or periodically.

Which brings us to the second word of the term, which is "intermittent." The key to making the practice of intentionally going hungry a great way to achieve better health and fitness (get and stay lean) is by doing it intermittently and not for very long periods of time, i.e., for days or week on end. Doing it this way doesn't just keep you from starving excessively to the point that your health suffers, but it can actually improve your health and help you live optimally.

To be more specific, here are intermittent fasting's top health benefits:

Accelerated Fat Loss

Losing weight isn't necessarily a great thing, especially if you lose the wrong kind of weight. Really? There's a right kind of weight loss? You bet there is, and it's called fat loss!

Many people confuse weight loss with fat loss, which is why so many unhealthy rapid weight loss diets – a.k.a. crash diets – continue to propagate on the Internet and beyond. While it's true that many crash diets can really make a person lose 10 pounds or more per week, it's worth noting that most of such weight lost is of the kind you don't want to lose: water and muscle mass.

Intermittent fasting helps you lose the right kind of

weight at a fast but healthy pace – body fat. Believe me, even if you just lose 2 pounds per week at most (the established healthy weight loss rate), 8 pounds of body fat in a month (at 4 weeks per month) will make you look significantly slimmer compared to 16 pounds in a month that's mostly water and muscle.

Why the need to preserve as much muscle mass as possible? The more muscle mass you have, the faster your metabolism is, i.e., the ability to burn calories consumed and stored body fat. When you lose mostly body fat and minimal muscle mass, your metabolism hardly changes and you'll continue burning mostly body fat the way forest fires rage through, well, forests!

Intermittent fasting helps speed up your metabolism by raising the production of fat-burning hormones such as norepinephrine while minimizing insulin production. It has been shown in studies that on average, intermittent fasting – if done right – can help your body burn up to 14% more calories and body fat. In particular, a review of a particular piece of scientific literature in 2014 showed that within 24 weeks, intermittent fasting can help people lose as much as 8% of their weight, which may be considered a substantial rate of weight loss for a relatively short period of time. Imagine if you're 200 pounds, you can lose as much as 16 pounds of mostly fat in just 6 months or less! In the same study, it was also discovered that the people who were involved in the study lost as much as 7% in terms of inches from their waistlines. This shows that most of the weight loss achieved was body fat.

In another study, intermittent fasting was shown to spare more muscle mass compared to calorie-restricted diets done over the long-term. The reason? Remember how intermittent fasting raises the production of fat-burning hormones while minimizing those of fat-inducing ones? Now you know why.

Because of its ability to limit your caloric consumption and improve your metabolism, intermittent fasting can help you achieve your weight loss, i.e., body fat loss, goals.

Minimize Type 2 Diabetes Risks

One of the world's fastest spreading health epidemics is diabetes. In many countries the world over, especially in affluent or 1st world countries, diabetes is turning out to be one of the deadliest medical conditions that governments are battling with. This medical condition is primarily the result of heightened insulin resistance (low insulin sensitivity), which makes a person's blood sugar consistently high to the point of being chronic. Conversely, the lower a person's resistance to insulin (high sensitivity) is, the lower his or her blood sugar usually is.

As mentioned earlier, intermittent fasting can help minimize the production of insulin. In several studies, it's been estimated that intermittent fasting can bring down insulin levels by as much as 31%. In the same vein, it was also estimated based on studies that intermittent fasting can help reduce blood sugar levels by as much as 6%.

By improving insulin sensitivity (decreasing insulin resistance) and lowering your blood sugar levels, intermittent fasting can help you minimize your risks for acquiring type-2 diabetes later in life. However, this benefit is more applicable for men than women. One study showed that on average, the blood sugar levels of women increased while on a 3-week intermittent fasting protocol.

Improved Cardiovascular Health

Today, ISIS or the Syrian Army isn't the world's number one killer. It is cardiovascular diseases. And there are health markers or risk factors that can help determine one's risks of heart disease.

One of intermittent fasting's likely benefits is the reduction of some of these markers or risk factors, which include elevated cholesterol levels, hypertension, blood sugar levels, triglyceride levels and markers for inflammation. I say "likely" because these benefits were mostly observed in animal subjects, which means there's a need for more studies to be conducted – this time on humans – concerning the cardiovascular benefits of intermittent fasting. Nevertheless, the likelihood of such benefits also holding true for humans is high considering that most scientific tests on the potential effects of drugs and other things are first tested on animals. And often times, the positive test results give researchers and scientists the go signal to apply such things on humans.

Improved Cellular Restoration

One process that's crucial for cellular repair is removal of waste from the cells, i.e., **autophagy.** This involves the metabolism of dysfunctional or broken proteins, which can build up in cells over time. Increased autophagy can help metabolize or remove more of such broken or dysfunctional proteins and consequently, improve your body's cellular repair function. Intermittent fasting can help your body achieve increased autophagy and in the process, help your body repair cells much better.

Cellular, Gene, And Hormonal Changes

When you haven't had anything to eat for a meaningful length of time, several important hormonal changes happen. This includes – as mentioned earlier – increased production of the fat burning hormone norepinephrine and reduction of insulin levels. As mentioned earlier too, it also includes increased autophagy that leads to better cellular repair.

Another hormonal change that can happen while fasting intermittently is increased production of human growth hormones, which can help you build more muscle or preserve muscle mass even while dieting. Aside from making you look much fitter, more muscle mass helps you become functionally stronger.

Reduced Levels of Oxidative Stress and Inflammation

The single biggest reason for premature aging and for most chronic and degenerative health conditions today is oxidative stress. **Why?** It's because it strikes your body where it's most important – at the cellular level! Oxidative stress involves the reaction of free radicals or unstable molecules with the body's crucial molecules like protein and DNA. And such reactions aren't good – they're harmful and damaging!

It has been demonstrated in scientific studies that intermittent fasting has the beneficial ability to help the body boost its ability to ward off or combat oxidative stress. Some studies have also revealed that intermittent fasting can also reduce another major factor for many chronic diseases: inflammation. Therefore, intermittent fasting is one of the best ways to slow down aging, and reduce your risks for many of today's chronic and **degenerative sicknesses.**

Better Management of Cancer

Some studies, albeit done on animals, have shown that intermittent fasting can help reduce risks for certain cancers through improved metabolic processes. When it comes to studies done on humans, intermittent fasting was shown to be helpful in **minimizing the side effects of chemotherapy.**

Optimal Mind

Many times, what's beneficial for the body in general is also beneficial for the brain. Better metabolism, substantial improvements in insulin and blood sugar levels, reductions in oxidative stress, and reduced inflammation can all contribute to optimal cognitive and mental performances as well as overall brain health. Animal studies have shown that intermittent fasting can help grow new nerve cells, which are crucial for optimal mental performance and brain health. Intermittent fasting has also been shown in other studies to stimulate production of brain-derived neurotropic factor (BDNF), an important hormone that can help reduce risks for mental problems like depression, among others. And lastly, intermittent fasting can also help minimize the damaging effects of strokes on one's brain.

Lower Risk for Alzheimer's disease

One of the world's most prevalent **neurodegenerative conditions** is Alzheimer's disease. Presently, there's still no known cure for Alzheimer's despite scientific breakthroughs that bring us closer to discovering such a cure. So at this point, the **best medicine is still prevention.**

While studies that have yielded significant findings on intermittent fasting's role in lowering the risk for Alzheimer's were conducted on animals, it doesn't mean intermittent fasting's anti-Alzheimer's benefits aren't applicable to humans. Remember, most scientific breakthroughs in the medical field were first validated in animals before humans. As such, it may be the case that intermittent fasting can help reduce one's risks for Alzheimer's disease and even for Parkinson's and Huntington's diseases. And while there aren't any significant studies done on humans as of now that validates intermittent fasting's role in the war against Alzheimer's, there are reports of Alzheimer's patients experiencing much better symptoms after fasting for a short period of time as an intervention method.

Generally Longer Life

Lastly, general improvements in overall health will consequently improve one's longevity. Because intermittent fasting can help bring about the aforementioned key health and fitness benefits, it's highly likely that incorporating intermittent fasting as part of a generally healthy lifestyle can help extend one's life.

Different Strokes, Different Strokes, Same Results

There are many ways to skin a cat, as the popular saying goes. When it comes to intermittent fasting, the same applies. In the next few chapters, we'll take a look at the most popular ways intermittent fasting is done all over the world, which are more commonly referred to as protocols. Each protocol has its own unique advantages, which can help you incorporate intermittent fasting into your lifestyle regardless of your personal circumstances.

Chapter 2: The Lean Gains Protocol

This is considered to be one of the world's **most popular** protocols for fasting intermittently. The proponent of this protocol is **Martin Berkhan** and the lean gains protocol's ideal for you if you love to hit the weights at the gym and want to get ripped and shredded, i.e., build muscle and lose body fat.

How It Works

If you're a man, you will need to fast for 16 hours every day and if you're a woman, you'll need to fast for a shorter period of time daily – 14 hours. The remaining 8 (men) to 10 (women) hours will be your feeding or eating window.

You don't totally go food-less during your 14-16 hour daily fasting period. You can still eat some food during those times except that you can only eat or drink stuff that's practically calorie free. On top of the list is of course, water! Other acceptable alternatives include calorie-free sodas and gums, unsweetened black coffee (or sweetened with a calorie-free sweetener like stevia), and tea.

Next to how long will you fast on the lean gains protocol is when should you schedule it within your day? It depends really but the best time would be when it's least difficult for you to fast. For most people, their ideal fasting time is throughout the evening – it's easier to fast when asleep – until late morning. For such people, late morning is normally 6 hours upon waking up.

If you're the type of person who has very hectic days most of the time, timing your eating window so that it corresponds to your days' busiest or most hectic times can help provide you with the necessary energy when you need it most. And scheduling your fasting period on your most "down" times will help you hold on to your fast.

More than just eating and not eating, you will also need to pay close attention to what you should and shouldn't eat during your feeding windows. In particular, you will need to consider that kinds of foods that are optimal for your regular workouts at the gym. On the days you'll be hitting the gym, you'll need more carbohydrates for fuel and less fat calories. But on days you won't be hitting the gym, more fat calories than carbs is better. **Why?** Fat calories are more satiating, i.e., more filling, which can help you feel fuller for longer and reduce your cravings or hunger during your fasting window. But regardless of whether or not you hit the gym, you must make sure to include adequate amounts of protein for muscle sparing or building.

Regardless of the type of calorie you'll be eating, it's important to eat whole and unprocessed foods most of the time. Once in a while, there's no harm in going for processed ones like a meal replacement shake or a granola bar, especially when you're in a tight fix. Just make sure that eating processed foods remain to be the exception rather than the norm.

Pros and Cons

As with all good things, this protocol has its own set of advantages and disadvantages. Let's talk about advantage first, foremost of which is that there'll be no fuss concerning the frequency of meals. Whether you eat everything in one sitting or 20 sittings, it doesn't matter as long as you eat within your designated feeding window only. For many people, the leeway to decide on how frequently to eat on a given day is a great blessing that allows them to really stick to intermittent fasting.

What the protocol gives by way of total freedom in choosing meal frequencies is often negated or mitigated by its relatively "strict" guideline on what types of calories to consume on a given day, i.e., more carbs than fat on workout days and more fats than carbs on non-workout days. For some people, this is quite cumbersome and thus, they fail to stick to the protocol altogether.

If you are receiving value from this book then please leave a <u>review</u> for it on Amazon.

Chapter 3: The Eat-Stop-Eat Protocol

This intermittent fasting protocol was created by a dude named **Brad Pilon.** If you're the type of person who's already eating right and healthy, then this may be the protocol for you. Compared to some of the relatively extreme eating protocols, the eat-stop-eat protocol's primarily hinged on moderation. What do I mean by that?

Here, you can eat pretty much anything you like for as long as you only eat moderate amounts of such. So if you want to eat a slice of pizza, go ahead! Just make sure you stick to that slice only and leave the rest of the other slices alone.

How It Works

With the eat-stop-eat method, you don't need to fast everyday. You'll only have to do it at most twice weekly for 24 hours each time. And during those 24-hour fasting periods, you can't eat anything but you may freely drink any beverage for as long as it doesn't have calories, e.g., water and green tea.

When your fasting period's done, you simply go back to your usual eating program. And according to the protocol's creator Brad Pilon, you can live as if you never fasted at all. With such leeway, different people break their fasts differently. Some just eat normally while others binge eat with one humongous meal. Still others do so by just enjoying a light snack. It's really up to you how you'd like to break your weekly fasts.

You also have the liberty of choosing the timing of your weekly fast or fasts. This means you can schedule your fast or fasts on days when you know you'll have the least difficult time fasting for 24 hours. For some people, it's the weekends while for some, it's when they're most busy at work so that they hardly become mindful of their being hungry. It's really up to you.

As mentioned earlier, this protocol's all about moderation. As such, it is one that aims to reduce your caloric consumption by reducing your meal frequency for the whole week, i.e., not eating for 1 or 2 days every week. By doing so, it inadvertently reduces your weekly caloric intake en route to fat loss.

Regular exercise is another important part of this particular protocol. In terms of such, weight lifting or resistance training exercises are the best ones to regularly perform. Why? It's because weight-training exercises are the best for at least maintaining or minimizing muscle mass loss while losing weight. And as I mentioned earlier, muscle mass is one of the most important factors that will determine how much calories your body can burn regularly and how much body fat you can lose while dieting.

Pros and Cons

When it comes to the Eat-Stop-Eat protocol, its biggest advantage is flexibility. Why? It's because this protocol lets you start small and take initially small but ever increasing steps towards full implementation. What this means is you don't need to put it all on the line and implement the protocol fully on your first day, which can be hard, especially when you haven't fasted your whole life. You can start by fasting for as long as you possibly can during the first day or two and gradually increasing the duration of your regular fasts as your body responds accordingly.

Brad Pilon – the protocol's creator and chief proponent – espouses that you start doing the protocol on your week's potentially busiest day or on a day where you don't have social gathering commitments to fulfill (minimize food temptations). By starting the protocol on a day that's characterized by at least one of the 2 conditions, you may be able to keep your mind too preoccupied to be conscious of food (or the lack of it), minimize the temptation to break your fast too early, or both.

Another **key benefit** of the protocol is that there is neither forbidden food items nor a duty to watch your calories like Golden State Warriors fans keep tabs on Steph Curry's 3-point shots made for the season. The fact that you don't need to strictly monitor what and how much you eat makes it substantially less difficult to implement this protocol compared to many other intermittent fasting methods. But nevertheless, it's important to keep in mind that this protocol isn't a license to buffet everyday like it's the end of the world. The key – as to anything else – is moderation. Eat anything you want but remember not to overdo it.

As for disadvantages, the only one associated with the Eat-Stop-Eat protocol is the duration of the fast, which is at least 24 hours. Whether, once or twice a week only, 24 hours without food can still be very challenging for most people especially during the first several weeks of implementation of the protocol, where side effects can be experienced. These can include being cranky, headaches, fatigue, or anxiety, which eventually fade away after the first several weeks.

If you choose to implement this protocol, know that the **24-hour** fast is a very challenging one, even if you gradually build up your fasting duration towards it. As such, the temptation to binge eat every time you break the fast can be very powerful. This is where you'll need to exert every ounce of willpower that you have to make sure you eat moderately when breaking your fasts under this protocol.

Chapter 4: The Warrior Diet Protocol

As the name suggests, this protocol requires you to eat like a **"warrior"**. And what does it mean to eat like one? For sure, it's not eating like the Golden State Warriors.

The protocol's creator, **Ori Hofmekler,** believes that warriors from the ancient times – particularly those training to be such – eat just 1 big meal everyday, which is dinner. For the rest of the 24 daily hours, these warriors fast. This particular protocol will suit you well if you're the type of person who is devoted to rules or a stickler for such.

How It Works

The diet is a **very simple one** – eat one large meal a day at night. That's it. Very simple isn't it? But why schedule your one big meal at night, which is contrary to what many conventional nutritional experts say? It's because according to Hofmekler, humans are naturally nocturnal or night eaters by genetic design. Given this particular genetic trait, it only makes sense to schedule your 1 big meal at night so that you can optimally feed your body with all the nutrients it needs as your body's circadian or sleep rhythm requires. Hofmekler explains that the reason for such is that doing so helps increase your parasympathetic nervous system's capacity to help your body relax, digest your food, recuperate, and calm down, all of which are conducive for maximum cellular repair and growth.

Further, Hofmekler claims that eating just one big meal in the evening can also help your body produce key hormones and consequently, burn more body fat during daytime. And when doing so, you will also need to consider the order by which you eat certain types of food during your 4-hour nighttime eating window. He recommends that you eat your veggies first, proteins next, and fats for last. And if despite your single big meal you're still hungry, you can eat some more carbs.

From the perspective of the Warrior Diet protocol, fasting is about eating below your means versus starvation. This perspective then allows you to actually eat during your fasting period, only that you eat small portions or servings of fruits, raw veggies, fresh juice, or protein. Doing this can help you boost your energy, optimize fat burning, and increase mental alertness throughout the day while fasting by increasing or boosting your sympathetic nervous system's flight-or-fight response.

Pros and Cons

The Warrior Diet protocol's main advantage is that technically speaking, it isn't a fast because it allows you to eat small portions of raw veggies, fruits, proteins, and juices during your 20-hour daily fasting period. As mentioned earlier, it's really more about under-eating more than starving yourself, which is what fasts are all about. This can make it much easier for you to implement consistently and stay on for the long term.

Other reported advantages of this protocol include significant improvements in energy levels and ability to burn body fat.

While the diet seems much easier to implement given you won't be starving yourself throughout your daily fasting periods of up to 20 hours, it can be challenging in terms of permitted foods to eat and eating schedule. Because you will be limited to veggies, lean proteins and good dietary fat and you can only eat a meal in the evening, it can prove to be rather challenging to attend most social gatherings while keeping strict compliance with the protocol.

Another potential disadvantage, particularly in the beginning, is the difficulty of eating practically all of your daily caloric requirements in the evening in just one sitting. This can be more pronounced considering most people are used to eating most of their daily food requirements during the day. But over time, this can be less challenging, as you gradually grow **accustomed to nocturnal eating.**

Chapter 5: The Alternate Day Protocol

This protocol was created by **Dr. James Johnson, MD.** Compared to the other intermittent fasting protocols, the Alternate Day diet may be considered one of the **easier protocols** to implement. It's because the protocol only requires you to fast every other day, i.e., you eat very little on your fasting days and eat normally in between days.

How It Works

It's worth clarifying what eating "very little" means because let's face it, the term means different things to different people. For **Shaquille O'Neal,** who stands 7 feet 1 inch tall and weighs 324 pounds, the term "very little" may already be considered as a buffet for Isaiah Thomas who stands just 5 feet 9 inches and weighs just a little over 185 pounds. So for purposes of this protocol, "very little" means getting just 20% of your daily caloric requirements or consumption. So if you're usually consuming **2,500 calories** a day, you only consume **500 calories** on your fasting days.

For convenience's sake, Dr. Johnson suggests drinking meal replacement shakes on the days that you fast. It's because such shakes can be easily consumed throughout the day and they can pack a lot of nutrients. But Dr. Johnson doesn't favor dependence on it. He says that past the first **2 weeks** of your starting the protocol, you must go back to eating real, whole foods during your fasting days.

And remember how we talked about regular weight lifting exercise being part of the warrior diet protocol? Weight lifting exercises are also a crucial part of the Alternate Day protocol. Because of that, the best time to schedule your workouts is on the days that you don't fast. Doing so will help you exert maximum effort doing your workouts and make the most out of them.

Pros and Cons

The alternate day protocol is one that's primarily focused on helping you lose the healthy kind of weight, which is body fat. If you lose more body fat than water or muscle mass in terms of weight, you won't just look and feel fit. You'll also be much healthier. Based on Dr. Johnson's website, you can lose as much as **2.5 pounds** weekly, which is what most health and fitness experts consider to be a safe weight loss pace.

Another advantage of this protocol is its relative

simplicity. No calorie counting or having to watch what you eat. It's one less stress on your mind.

But its relative simplicity can also be a disadvantage in that you severely cut your calories every other day to only **20%** of your usual, which can be too much if you're not used to fasting. While it may be simple to practically eat nothing the whole day every other day, it's not the easiest thing in the world to do. And it's higher than normal level of difficulty can make your risks for binge eating on normal days much higher. That's unless you have a very strong will power or you can effectively plan your activities far ahead in advance to ensure that you minimize temptations for eating more than that which is required on both your fasting and normal eating days.

Chapter 6: The Fat Loss Forever Protocol

This intermittent fasting protocol was developed by **Dan Go** and **John Romaniello.** If you're a gym rat who thinks of diet cheat days as God's greatest gift to gym rats, then this protocol may be the ideal one for you. Why?

One reason is that it brings together the best of the Lean Gains, Eat-Stop-Eat, and Warrior Diet protocols in just one. Think of it as a pack of 3-in-1 coffee only that it's intermittent fasting.

Two of its major features is a push and pull sort of relationship between heaven and hell, where you get 1 whole day for cheat meals every week (heaven) followed by a 36-hour fast (hell). The 5 other days are then divided among the 3 different protocols according to your preference.

The protocols creators suggest that you schedule your longest fasting period on the days that you're busiest. Why? So that your mind will be too preoccupied to think about or notice the hunger that's brewing in your stomach. You can buy the protocol's plan on Dan and John's website and get free training programs (bodyweight and free weight exercises), which can help you make the most out of your healthy weight loss (fat loss) efforts.

Pros and Cons

Its most significant pro is that the **7-day** cycle for fasting lets your body acclimatize to a fasting table that has a structure. As a result, you can maximize the fat burning and muscle-building results of the protocol and your training program. Per Dan and John, everybody fasts on a daily basis. The only difference is how they do it, e.g., others do it carelessly. With the Fat Loss Forever protocol, you can fast in a highly structured, controlled, and effective manner.

Its disadvantage? Well, it's similar to the other protocols in that after the longest fast of the week, i.e., **36 hours,** the temptation to binge eat as you break that fast is very high compared to other protocols given that you fasted for a significantly longer period of time.

Another potential disadvantage of the protocol – at least at first – is that it can be quite confusing or challenging to follow strictly. Why? It's because of its strict but widely varying schedules throughout the 7-day cycle. Remember that for **5** days, you'll be doing the 3 protocols we mentioned earlier, which can keep you from establishing a rhythm or pattern. But as you progress along with the protocol, you'll eventually get used to it.

Chapter 7: The 5:2 Diet Protocol

Also referred to as **The Fast Diet,** the 5:2 protocol is one of the most, if not the most, popular of the intermittent fasting protocols these days. Why?

How It Works

The protocol – made popular by British journalist and **Doctor Michael Mosley** – lets people eat normally for 5 days in a week and fast for only 2 days. Now you may be wondering, isn't this how the Eat-Stop-Eat method works? On the surface, it seems so. But actually, they work differently.

For one, you can fast just one day during the week with the Eat-Stop-Eat protocol while under the 5:2 protocol, you fast for 2 days. Another key difference is that you can actually eat during the 2 fasting days under the 5:2 protocol while in the Eat-Stop-Eat method, you can only enjoy calorie free drinks while fasting.

Speaking of calories, you're allowed to consume a total of **500 calories** if you're a woman or **600 calories** if you're a man on your fasting days. There are no "rules" as to what you can and can't eat or when you should eat during your fasting days. But if you want to minimize the stress, you can follow the lead of many people who've already done the 5:2 Diet protocol, which is to follow one of the 2 fasting patterns:

- Three (3) mini-meals, one each over breakfast, lunch, and dinner; or
- Two (2) smaller than normal meals, normally over lunch and dinner.

Remember that the only rule here is to limit caloric intake to a maximum of **600** and **500** calories if you're a man or a woman, respectively, throughout your fasting day. Therefore, you should budget your calories wisely across the day.

While there's no "right" or "wrong" foods under this protocol, there are wise and unwise choices. Going for food items that are high in fiber and protein are generally wise choices as these help you feel full for longer and can significantly reduce hunger pangs. In turn, those can help you keep your calories to within the daily limit.

Another wise food choice are soups made from whole food ingredients. Don't go for commercially available and synthetic "instant" soups. They're neither good for your health nor your waistline.

The only other rule you'll need to abide by under this protocol is to ensure that there's at least 1 normal eating day in between your **2** days of weekly fasting. Many people who do this protocol schedule their fasting days every Monday and Thursday, eating **3** small meals on each of those days, and eating normally for the remaining days.

And speaking of eating normally, please don't confuse it with "buffet" or eating as much as you can. Normally means just that, normal. Eat the same amount as you normally would when you're not fasting.

Pros and Cons

One of the advantages of this protocol is that it doesn't really feel like a diet because it's more an eating pattern than a "fast". Not only do you get to eat small portions of food on your fasting days, which is only for 2 days every week, but you also have no restrictions as to the kinds of foods to eat. As such, many people feel it's much easier to stick to this protocol than most other intermittent fasting protocols or weight loss diets for that matter.

The only **disadvantage of this protocol** in my viewpoint is that you won't lose as much weight as most of the others given it's more lenient in terms of caloric consumption. Your fasting days are more like "severe calorie restriction" days rather than non-eating days. But if you feel you're not hardcore enough to lose more weight on the other harder protocols, it's alright. To each his own and if this protocol suits you best, then by all means go for it.

Chapter 8: The Spontaneous Fasting Protocol

The last protocol we'll be looking at is what I'd consider to be Intermittent Fasting Lite because it's the **easiest of all protocols.** Why?

How It Works

As the name suggests, there are no rules as to when you'll fast. Fasting under this protocol is pretty much like watching movies on **Netflix,** i.e., on demand. Here, you won't have to stick to a particular structure for fasting intermittently. You just fast on the go and off the fly! Just skip meals every now and then, especially when you're not hungry yet or have so much to do that you can't afford to eat. Just make sure you get to eat nutritious and healthy meals when you do decide to eat.

In a nutshell, the spontaneous fasting protocol is a more organic way of fasting intermittently by skipping one or 2 meals daily when it's most convenient.

Pros and Cons

Obviously, its greatest advantage is the lack of structure. You can skip your meals at your most convenient times of the day and there are no forbidden foods. As such, there's really no reason for you not to be able to fast intermittently except for one: you don't really want to do it.

Its greatest advantage can also be its biggest disadvantage. Some people need structure in order to get things done and if you're such a person, the lack of structure of this diet can make it hard for you to successfully implement it.

Another disadvantage of this intermittent fasting protocol is that being the easiest one to do, it may also reap the least beneficial results, especially when it comes to healthy weight loss. Let's face it, healthy weight loss is still all about calorie reduction and being in a consistent state of caloric deficits, i.e., calories consumed are less than calories used or burned. A protocol that's not predicated on any consistent effort for significantly reducing calories is one that may keep you from optimal weight or fat loss. It's either you lose significant weight much longer than the other protocols or you lose significantly less weight for a given period of time compared to the other protocols. Such is the trade-off between convenience and results.

Chapter 9: Muscles – The Secret to Getting and Staying Lean

When it comes to healthy weight loss, i.e., body fat loss, nutrition or diet is just part of the equation. Another crucial aspect – maybe an even more important one – is metabolism or the rate at which your body's able to burn calories or body fat. Obviously, the higher your metabolism is, the more calories or body fat your body can burn. So a fast metabolism coupled with calorie reduction is a potent one-two punch against body fat.

And when it comes to metabolism, one of the most important factors affecting it is the amount of muscle mass your body has. Why? Of all your body's cells, muscles are the most metabolically active, i.e., require the most calories for normal functioning. It therefore follows that the more muscle mass you have, the faster your metabolism can be and consequently, your metabolism slows down when your muscle mass is reduced.

When it comes to maintaining or even increasing muscle mass while fasting intermittently, there's a lot of "passionate" discussions going around. Many who take the conventional point of view say that severe caloric restriction – as is the case when fasting – leads to breaking down of muscle tissue and consequently, to muscle loss. But just how true are statements like these?

To answer that question, we'll need to consider 2 things. First is the kind of calories you consume. The second is the timing of the consumption, i.e. when you eat them. The following practical tips will help you address these 2 factors in ways that will allow you to maintain or even increase muscle mass even while fasting intermittently.

Eat Breakfast

Whether as a means by which to break your fast or a way to begin it, aim to eat something in the morning according to your chosen fasting schedule. If you choose to fast at night, then break your fast in the day with a – pardon the pun – small breakfast to launch your day on an energized note. If you choose to fast during the day, do the same, i.e., eat a small breakfast just before your fasting period begins to start the day somewhat energized as well.

But considering that you want to keep an optimal metabolism through muscle mass, building or maintaining muscle mass must be your primary focus or priority. And whether you choose to fast during the day or all throughout the night, one great way to keep your muscles well-nourished and primed up for growth or maintenance is by eating something the moment you wake up.

So what's the best food to eat in the morning for optimal muscle maintenance or growth? As much as possible, go for proteins that are slow to digest such as cheese, red meat, and eggs. **Why?** More than just making you feel satiated for much longer, they provide your muscles with the primary building blocks for growth or maintenance – protein. And aside from protein, you'll also benefit from eating some carbohydrates as it can help your mental and physical performance during the day.

When it comes to the timing of your fasting period, there's only 1 significant difference, which is the ability to spread out your caloric consumption. If you fast in the evening, you can spread out your caloric consumption throughout the full range of your eating window because you're awake. If you choose to fast during the day, you only get to eat your total calories for the 24-hour period in one big meal at night. That's unless you fancy waking up in the middle of the night to spread out your daily caloric consumption over several meals.

Schedule Your Workouts Later In the Day

Before you hit the weights, or perform bodyweight exercises such as **plyometrics or calisthenics,** it's paramount that you're able to get in a significant amount of calories in order to perform your exercises well and not faint from exhaustion. And hitting the gym, or doing calisthenics or plyometrics later in the day can help you do those regardless if you choose to fast during the day or night.

If you go for daytime fasting that ends late in the afternoon or early evening, say at 6 p.m., it will do you well to schedule your workouts later in the evening after you've gotten the chance to eat something. Aside from having enough energy, working out later in the evening increases your odds of using the machines you fancy as most people would've been done with their workouts, leaving you with very little competition for gym equipment.

If you choose to fast at night, working out late in the afternoon or early evening's your best bet. So if you start your fast at 5 or 6 in the afternoon, your best bet for working out is at 4 or 5 p.m., respectively. Doing so gives you just the opportunity to get your final calories in before and immediately after your workout just prior to starting your fasting period.

You may think, why not work out in the middle of the day? It's not a good idea especially if you fast during the day because you won't have the opportunity to get enough calories in for a meaningful workout. If you choose to work out in the morning, it'll be too cumbersome especially if you have a day job.

Eat After Working Out

Lastly, you should do your best to schedule the consumption of the bulk of your daily calories immediately after your workouts. Why? It's because of what's referred to as the **2-hour golden post-workout window** wherein your body's ability to recover and build muscle can be maximized via immediate post-workout nutrients. And more importantly, your body's chances of storing all those extra calories from post-workout meals are at its lowest during this golden window because your body, particularly your muscles, need all the protein it can get for rebuilding and all the carbohydrates it can get to quickly replenish its glycogen stores, i.e., it's primary fuel. And eating too much just before working out increases your chances of feeling lethargic and sluggish while exercising.

Chapter 10: Practical Tips for Intermittent Fasting Success

Make no mistake about it, intermittent fasting is one of the most effective method for getting into the best shape of your life and improving your health. However, it's not something that works for everyone, i.e., a one-size-works-for-all thing. For some people, intermittent fasting may even be detrimental to their health if they have pre-existing chronic sicknesses, medical issues, or special dietary needs. If you're one of them, it's best to check with your doctor first to see if intermittent fasting won't be harmful to you given your medical condition or unique dietary needs.

Assuming that you're generally healthy and have no special nutritional requirements, you must be very sensitive to the signals your body may give if you decide to fast intermittently. You must be able to sense if your body's legitimately screaming for help and get appropriate medical help, or if it's just complaining about how uncomfortable intermittent fasting is during the first few weeks. Let's face it — most people don't consider intermittent fasting "normal" and because of that, it will really take some time to acclimatize to the lifestyle. And for women, volatile hormonal levels can make it much more challenging to start and stay on any intermittent fasting protocol compared to men.

When it comes to intermittent fasting, you're better off being prudent by being careful or cautious in the beginning and gradually transitioning from short periods of fasting to much longer durations. If despite your best efforts and several weeks into the lifestyle you still feel very uncomfortable, there's no shame in accepting that intermittent fasting may not be for you and that other nutritional approaches may be your thing. Not being able to fast intermittently as a lifestyle won't erode your value as a person.

In order to maximize your chances of successfully transitioning to the intermittent fasting lifestyle, consider the following practical tips for starting the lifestyle.

Water

While you're in a fasting phase or period, one of the most – if not the most – important things you'll need is water. Unfortunately, many people who are into the intermittent fasting lifestyle are frequently dehydrated. And being frequently dehydrated while on any intermittent fasting protocol is bad for you. Why?

Your body is primarily made up of water. Yes, up to 70% of your body's made up of the stuff and as such, substantial drops in your body's water levels can have subtle but substantial impact on your cells and nerves that can impede optimal mental and physical performance.

Chronic dehydration can also make you susceptible to dizziness, constipation, dry skin, and fatigue, among others. And when you're fasting, you should stick to drinking pure water for hydration because anything else may contain high amounts of sugar and hidden calories, even if the labels say "sugar free" or "zero calories".

Another reason why you need to get enough water for healthy weight loss while fasting intermittently regardless of your chosen protocol is that it helps you feel fuller for longer. That's why even during the night, it's important that you still get to drink a glass or two of water, particularly when you're fasting. It helps you minimize hunger pangs.

So how much water is enough water? It's best to get more than **8 glasses daily** since you're fasting intermittently, and even more importantly if you're exercising regularly. And make sure that you spread out your water over several drinks throughout the day and night instead of just one or two drinks. Believe me, drinking your daily water requirements in just one or two sittings can be very uncomfortable to do regularly.

While drinking very cold water is very refreshing especially on hot days or nights, you'd be better off drinking room temperature or slightly cold water. **Why?** It's because very cold water can stimulate contraction in your blood vessels and cause indigestion.

The foods you choose to eat within your feeding windows may also impact your hydration levels. One of the foods you should minimize or avoid altogether are spicy ones because of their tendency to make you much thirstier. Salt is an ingredient that can make you significantly thirstier than usual so keep your consumption of very salty food to a minimum. And if you do eat very salty food, make sure to increase your water intake in order to lessen the relatively strong taste.

You can increase your chances of being adequately hydrated by eating fruits and veggies that are fibrous and loaded with water. More than just helping you with hydration, they also have the effect of making you feel fuller for longer.

And if you want to enjoy a glass or two of fruit juice, don't go for commercially available ones, no matter how much manufacturers claim them to be **"all natural"**. Truth is, commercially available fruit juices are laden with sugar so you're best bet is to drink freshly squeezed or pressed fruit juice. That way, you can be 100% sure that what you're drinking doesn't contain excess sugar or other harmful ingredients.

Scheduling Your Fast

The timing of your fasting periods can be a significant factor in terms of you being able to do intermittent fasting long enough to experience its benefits. This can be even more crucial if you choose to maximize fat loss through regular workouts at the gym.

Many people who fast intermittently have day jobs and other big responsibilities to take care of. That's why for them, choosing the optimal time for their fasting phases is of prime importance. That's why most people tend to schedule their fasting periods throughout the evening and into the morning. By doing so, they're able to feed themselves when they need to the most, which is during the day, and fast when energy expenditure's lowest, i.e., throughout the night. So if you're seriously considering getting into the intermittent fasting lifestyle, consider timing your fasts in the evening, where the risk of breaking your fast prematurely is at its lowest.

Lift Weights

Exercise that's called by any other name – contrary to popular notion – will neither burn the same amount of body fat nor make you look healthy and fit. That's why in case you still haven't noticed, I keep on promoting weight lifting or resistance exercises, including calisthenics and plyometrics, as the primary mode of regular exercise. And again, the reason behind it is that resistance or weight lifting exercises are best for both burning fat and building muscle.

I've seen friends who only dieted without exercising and when they lost weight, they look like they contracted some serious sickness. While they lost weight, they didn't look fit. They looked weak and frail because most of their weight loss was water and worse, muscle mass.

Contrast it to my friends and myself who have lost some weight but looked as fit as hell. How'd that happen despite not losing as much "weight" as my pure-diet-friends? It's because while we lost much body fat, we also gained muscle mass, which kind of ate into the total weight loss figure. That's why despite losing less pounds than my pure-diet friends, we looked like we lost more weight and looked much fitter and stronger.

And when it comes to resistance or weight lifting exercises, please don't think you need to be a power lifter or bodybuilder, or perform their grueling workouts. Those guys and gals are extreme and

257

chances are, your body won't be able to handle it. All you need to do is perform basic compound lifts such as deadlifts, bench presses, and squats using enough weight where you reach failure, i.e., can no longer lift the weight, for a 9th straight repetition. Do **3 sets of 8 reps** max for each weight lifting exercise for optimal muscle training.

If you don't have access to a gym or a set of weights, you can perform bodyweight exercises such as plyometrics and calisthenics instead. Your body is a good weight to work with. Start with the number of reps you can do for each exercise and gradually build up to 12 reps per set, going for at least 2 sets per exercise.

Chapter 11: Top Mistakes to Avoid When Fasting Intermittently

Doing things right is just half the battle. The other half is avoiding mistakes that can derail your success, especially the crucial ones. And when it comes to intermittent fasting for weight, loss, health, and energy, it's the same. That's why in this final chapter, we'll discuss the top mistakes that can keep you from succeeding at intermittent fasting and how to avoid them.

Eating the Wrong Foods

Many folks who claim to have faithfully complied with intermittent fasting's guidelines and protocols don't have the bodies to show for it. Why's that so, considering they've reportedly stuck to their fasting and eating windows like bubble gum sticks to hair? If you ask them what they normally eat during their feeding windows, you'd be shocked to hear their answers: they eat mostly processed and junk foods.

There's a saying that garbage in, garbage out. When it comes to getting into great shape and health, nothing else is as true. What you eat will ultimately determine how you look and feel. No intermittent fasting protocol will ever cut it for you if you eat like crap.

Yes, there are a few very gifted people who seem to be exempted from this curse of garbage-eat-garbage-body. And they're the very few exceptions to the rule. So don't for one second take for granted that you're one of them. Unless there's compelling evidence that you are, you're not. You should take great care in choosing the foods you will regularly eat and you shouldn't leave your diet to chance.

So how does it look like to eat healthy? For one, healthy eating means eating mostly whole or "natural" foods, i.e., foods that are as close to their original states as possible. The more processed a food is, i.e., the farther it looks from its original form, the more unhealthy ingredients have been added to them, many of which won't just keep you fat but also make you sick over the long term.

So how do whole foods look like? Grilled chicken, steak, and pork chops are natural or whole foods because they haven't changed from their original form. On the other hand, burgers, hotdogs, and chicken nuggets are some of the best examples of processed foods, the consumptions of which you must minimize for health and fitness purposes. Other examples of highly processed foods are bagels, donuts, cookies...and the list goes on!

Another type of food you must minimize or even avoid altogether are sugar-filled foods and drinks. Not only are these calorie dense, i.e., pack a lot of calories for little volume, they also put you at risk for screwed up metabolism and diabetes. Stick to pure water, green tea or unsweetened coffee for drinks and fruits, veggies, and brown rice for carbs instead.

So Much Free Time

There's a saying that idle hands are the devil's workshop. In a practical sense, it's true because when you have so much time on your hands, you will tend to fill it up with anything that's within reach. It's because people aren't wired to do nothing – we'll always look for something to fill up our time with. And often times, the most proximate or convenient way to fill up vacant time is through sedentary activities and food. Worse, junk and processed foods are the most convenient types around.

In order to avoid falling into this trap, I'm not suggesting that you fill up each and every second of your free time and refuse to have much needed down time. The keyword here is excessive because beyond what you really need for regular rest and relaxation lie the strongest temptations for all things unhealthy and fattening.

One of the best ways to minimize your risks for falling into this trap is to begin your intermittent fasting on a day that you perceive will be a very busy one. When you do that, your mind will be too preoccupied with all the things you need to do to the point that it won't be as conscious of the substantial dietary changes involved. If you start your intermittent fasting journey on a lazy day at home, your risk for breaking the fast prematurely on the first day is high because most if not all of your attention will be focused on nothing else but your hunger.

Overdosing On Stimulants

Caffeine's been scientifically proven to help optimize physical and mental performance by, among others, increasing your heart rate and making you feel awake. As a result, it can also help you burn more body fat when fasting intermittently.

But while it can be a great thing, all things good or great can be detrimental once taken excessively. A cup or two of your favorite unsweetened black coffee or green tea can be very helpful during the day, but drinking 3 or more on a regular basis isn't. Because of its acidic nature, drinking excessive caffeine can make you feel much hungrier than you really are and make it really hard for you to stay on your fast.

Too much caffeine will also rob you of a great night's

rest, which is even more important if you're fasting intermittently. Lack of quality sleep will make you feel weak, sluggish, and hazy during the day, all of which substantially increases your risk for overcompensation with – you guessed it right – food! As a good general guideline, your last cup should be at 3 in the afternoon at the latest. That should give your body enough time to flush out the caffeine from your system so you can get a great night's sleep.

Setting Goals That Are Too Lofty

One way that you can fail even before you start fasting intermittently is by setting unrealistic goals for yourself on your fast. When you do that, you're merely setting yourself up to fail big time. And such hard failures can knock the wind out of you to the point that you'd want to ditch intermittent fasting altogether.

When aiming to achieve personal goals, the wise thing to do is set smaller, more realistic goals that build up towards your major ones. But these goals need to be challenging as well. Why? If they're not challenging, accomplishing them won't mean anything to you and that means you won't be encouraged to aim for the next higher ones. If you set smaller, realistic and challenging goals, you set yourself up to experience small but major victories that will build up your confidence in achieving bigger goals.

How does this look like for intermittent fasting? Instead of aiming to be able to fast 16 hours straight, make it your first goal to skip 1 major meal a day, i.e., lunch, or dinner. If that's too big for you, try skipping snacks first before going to the major meals. That way, you don't shock your body by going cold turkey on food. And by gradually building up the duration of your fasting periods, you get to build up your capacity and confidence to fast for substantially longer periods of time.

Another example is weight loss. If you need to lose a total of 50 pounds, don't make it your goal to lose 50 pounds right off the bat. Start by making it your goal to lose 10 pounds over 2 months first. Once you get that out of the way, aim for the next 10 pounds, and so on until you eventually reach 50 pounds.

Fear of the Empty Stomach

The biggest fear of many dieters, especially those who want to embrace the intermittent fasting lifestyle, is the fear of going hungry as if it's the devil's child. Hunger is nothing but another part of normal, everyday living and unlike what many nutrition and fitness "gurus" preach, intermittent fasting won't lead to muscle wastage or loss if done right. You also won't die prematurely after fasting for 24 hours unless you've been fasting for 30 days already!

As mentioned in Chapter 1, purposefully going hungry through proper intermittent fasting protocols can actually be very beneficial for your health and overall fitness. If intermittent fasting is a sure way to shrivel your muscles away and die from hunger, why does regular or intermittent fasting play a major part in the lives of millions of people all over the world who still happen to be alive, alert, awake, and enthusiastic?

Continuously going hungry for excessive periods of time is unhealthy or even downright dangerous. But that's not what intermittent fasting is. The word "intermittent" means among other things sporadic, irregular, or erratic. In other words, intermittent implies something that's not continuous or long lasting. It's a stop-and-go thing. By going hungry intermittently, you won't go to the extreme of starving to death.

Being Overly Cautious

There's an important principle in finance – particularly investments – that may also be applied to intermittent fasting. It says that if you want to earn higher returns or profits, you'll need to take higher risks or more volatility. And according to Mr. Hofmekler (remember him of the Warrior Diet fame?), volatility is your best friend when it comes to effective intermittent fasting. To cut all the technical mumbo-jumbo, Hofmekler claims that the nutrients you consume or ingest become even more beneficial or powerful if your body doesn't get them regularly, i.e., consumption is unpredictable. When you start to fast intermittently, you actually break the predictable nutrient consumption pattern that your body's been used to for practically your whole life. And with such unpredictability comes greater results.

Looking at "hunger" in a negative light can make you overly cautious and avoid it at all costs. But as with investments, you'll need to take bolder, riskier steps if you want to achieve greater returns. In this case, you will need to put down some of your personal walls that can keep you from embracing sporadically purposeful hunger as your ally. By taking the risk of intentionally going hungry, you'll break your body's predictable feeding pattern and in the process, you'll significantly increase the nutritional benefits it gets from the foods you'll eat.

Much Ado about Timelines

No doubt about it – the duration of your fast and how you time them are important aspects of intermittent fasting. But that doesn't mean you should be obsessed with timing because being so can just stress you out and negate or mitigate your chances of successfully achieving your fitness and health goals through intermittent fasting. You should take it seriously, no doubt about it, but you shouldn't overdo it. You must also learn how to relax.

So how can you tell if you're obsessed about timelines? If you easily get stressed over instances when you aren't able to fast or feed at your appointed "right" times, then you probably are. While you should do your best to stick to your appointed feasting and fasting periods, being off by minutes won't derail your efforts to lose body fat and achieve great health.

Looking At Individual Components Instead Of the Overall Picture

The word synergy implies that the whole is greater than the sum of its parts. Now what does that mean in layman's terms? With synergy, 5 plus 5 equals 15! Without synergy, or using the simple arithmetic method, 5 plus 5 is just 10, which is the sum of its parts.

When it comes to intermittent fasting, the beneficial results are due to the synergistic interactions of its different aspects. Intermittent fasting doesn't work on a per aspect or component basis – they work as a team. It's a holistic endeavor. Focusing on just one or two components, e.g., fasting, feeding, or hydration, won't get you very far. You may just find yourself greatly disappointed when you fail to achieve your weight loss and health goals and consequently, ditch the whole thing.

So when you start fasting intermittently, always remember that it's all about synergy between its important components, i.e., fasting periods, feasting periods, timing, quality of food eaten, hydration, getting enough quality sleep, getting regular exercise and incorporating key practices into your lifestyle. When you look at the overall picture, you become less obsessed with each component and significantly increase your chances of sticking to your chosen protocol and achieve your weight loss and health goals.

A "Diet" Perspective

Lastly, the intermittent fasting practice isn't just a "diet" but a **lifestyle.** What this means is that it isn't something you just go all out on for a few weeks or months before ditching to go back to your previous eating habits. It's a way of life.

When you look at it from such a short-term perspective, you commit 2 other mistakes that can sabotage your efforts to achieve your desired body weight and good health. The first of these mistakes is that you may go to the extreme of being obsessed with intermittent fasting to the neglect of other important areas of your life like family, friends, and work, among others. Doing so can make you miss out on many of life's greatest joys and when you do, you may eventually blame intermittent fasting for it and ditch it altogether.

The second mistake that you may commit by looking at intermittent fasting as more of a diet rather than a healthy eating lifestyle is binge eating as soon as you're done with the diet. If you'll put everything on the line to go all out with intermittent fasting for a short period of time, you'll put yourself at high risk for recovering all the "lost eating opportunities" when you're done with it. And in most cases, people who binge eat right after dieting successfully tend to not only gain back the weight they lost but also add more pounds to their previously heavy weight.

When you look at intermittent fasting as a lifestyle, you will inadvertently consider all the other important aspects of a healthy lifestyle and increase your chances of not just fasting intermittently over the long haul but achieving your fitness and health goals.

<u>Conclusion</u>

As you've learned in this book, intermittent fasting is one of the best ways to get into great shape and good health. You also learned the different ways of fasting intermittently – a.k.a. protocols – and saw that regardless of your personal circumstances or schedule, you can incorporate it as part of your overall lifestyle. The only exception would be is if you have a preexisting medical condition or special nutritional needs. But other than that, intermittent fasting can be a sustainable eating lifestyle that can contribute greatly to a fulfilling life.

But knowing is just half the battle of losing weight and achieving good health. The other half is action or application of knowledge. As such, I strongly encourage you to start applying what you learned in this book as soon as possible. And as I mentioned in some of the chapters, you neither have to apply everything all at once nor go cold turkey on food. Take baby steps and gradually build yourself up in terms of living the intermittent fasting lifestyle. By doing that, you significantly raise your chances of successfully incorporating it into your lifestyle and keep it there. And of course, you increase your chances of enjoying its key benefits – healthy weight loss and good health.

From The Author

Thank you for purchasing this bundle of three books. I hope you must have received value from these books. The purpose of putting these books together in a bundle was just to provide you with everything you need in one place. Intermittent Fasting when followed with Ketogenic diet is very effective and the weight loss is rapid. In some cases, you might not see immediate effects but don't worry, not everyone has the same metabolism and genetics. Just be patient and follow the knowledge you have gained from these books.

I hope that you'll apply the knowledge that you've gained from these books and you'll achieve Health Mastery.

If you need more recipe ideas for Desserts, Soups, Ice Creams, Fast Food, Side Dishes. You can check out my Author Page on Amazon: "John T. Smith"

If you have any queries or questions related to your health or anything taught in these books, then you can contact me anytime at my email. I would love to hear from you.

Cheers!

77900135R00152

Made in the USA
Lexington, KY
03 January 2018